GIRL
IN A
LIBRARY

ALSO BY KELLY CHERRY

POETRY
Hazard and Prospect: New and Selected Poems
Rising Venus
Death and Transfiguration
God's Loud Hand
Natural Theology
Relativity: A Point of View
Lovers and Agnostics

FICTION
We Can Still Be Friends
The Society of Friends
My Life and Dr. Joyce Brothers
The Lost Traveller's Dream
In the Wink of an Eye
Augusta Played
Sick and Full of Burning

NONFICTION
History, Passion, Freedom, Death, and Hope: Prose about Poetry
Writing the World
The Exiled Heart: A Meditative Autobiography

LIMITED EDITIONS
The Globe and the Brain, an essay
Welsh Table Talk, a poem sequence
An Other Woman, a poem
The Poem, an essay
Time out of Mind, poems
Benjamin John, a poem sequence
Songs for a Soviet Composer, a poem cycle
Conversion, a story

TRANSLATION
Antigone, *in* Sophocles, 2
Octavia, *in* Seneca: The Tragedies, Volume II

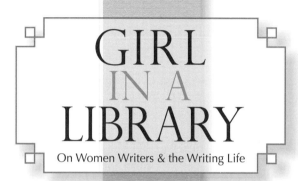

GIRL
IN A
LIBRARY

On Women Writers & the Writing Life

KELLY CHERRY

BkMk Press
University of Missouri-Kansas City

BkMk Press
University of Missouri-Kansas City
5101 Rockhill Road
Kansas City, Missouri 64110
(816) 235-2558 (voice) / (816) 235-2611 (fax)
www.umkc.edu/bkmk

Missouri Arts Council
The State of the Arts

Financial assistance for this project has been provided by
the Missouri Arts Council, a state agency.

Cover design: Cara Lefebvre
Book interior design: Susan L. Schurman
Managing editor: Ben Furnish

BkMk Press wishes to thank Gina Padberg, Elizabeth Gromling.
Special thanks to Cara Lefebvre, Shane Stricker, Molly Lesher.

12 lines from "Man and Wife" from *Collected Poems* by Robert Lowell.
Copyright © 2003 by Harriet Lowell and Sheridan Lowell. Reprinted by
permission of Farrar, Straus and Giroux, LLC.

Library of Congress Cataloguing-in-Publication Data

Cherry, Kelly
    Girl in a library: on women writers and the writing life / Kelly
Cherry.
        p. cm.
    ISBN 9781886157668 (pbk. : alk. paper)
Includes index.
Cherry, Kelly. Women authors, American -- 20th century -- Biography.
PS3553.H357 Z67 2009
818/.5409 B 22
                                2009019815

This book is set in Adobe Jenson Pro, Perpetua Titling.
Printed by McNaughton & Gunn.
Second printing 2012

To my wonderful sister, Ann,
and all my sisters in art

ACKNOWLEDGMENTS

Some of the essays and reviews collected herein have been previously published, sometimes under other titles and in earlier versions. "Why I Write" appeared in *The North American Review* 274.4 (1989). "I Was a Teenage Beatnik" appeared in *The Southern Review* 36.4 (2000) and was reprinted in *Knoxville Bound: A Literary Anthology*, ed. Dennis McCarthy (Knoxville, TN: Metro Pulse Publishing, 2004). "The Beauty Mark" appeared in *Living Fit* (May 1997). "My Mother and Mr. Allen Dewey Spooner" appeared in *The Chattahoochee Review* 13.3 (1993) and was reprinted in *Guide to Writing Magazine Nonfiction*, ed. Michael Bugeja (1998). "The Meaning of Guilt" appeared in *The Southern Review* 28.1 (1992). "Self and Strangeness" appeared in *Alabama Literary Review* 14.1 (2000). Portions of "Fictions by Four Contemporary African American Women Writers" appeared in *The Chicago Tribune Book World* (1975), *The American Book Review* (1988), and *The Los Angeles Times Book Review* (1992 , 1994). "Art We Cannot Live Without: Mary Ward Brown" appeared in *The Hollins Critic* 40.4 (2003). "Self and Sensibility: Elizabeth Hardwick" appeared in *The Hollins Critic* 36.2 (1999) and was reprinted in *Twayne Companion to Contemporary Literature in English: From the Editors of The Hollins Critic*, ed. R. H. W. Dillard and Amanda Cockrell (New York: Twayne Publishers, 2003). "Literary Theory and the Actual Writer" appeared in *New Literary History* 21 (1989). "The Daresomeness of a Southern Woman Writer" appeared in *America* October 23, 1999. "The Globe and the Brain: On Place in Fiction" was delivered as the Wallace Stegner Lecture at Lewis-Clark State College and published as a chapbook with that title by Talking River Publications (2006). A portion of "What Comes Next" appeared in *The Independent on Sunday* (London), (1993), a shortened version of the whole was published in *Writers on Writing: The Art of the Short Story*, ed. Maurice A. Lee (Westport: Praeger, 2004), and the essay appeared, in its entirety, in *Crafting Fiction, Poetry, and Memoir*, ed. Matthew Leone (Hamilton, NY: Colgate University Press, 2008). "Called to It" appeared in *Contemporary Authors* Vol. 209 (Gale Publishing, 2003) as part of the Gale Autobiography Series. I am grateful to the editors and publishers for presenting these essays and reviews to the public.

I am especially grateful to my editor at BkMk Press, Ben Furnish, for his warm support and friendly and helpful suggestions and for pointing out to me that this is a book about reading.

GIRL
IN A
LIBRARY

"I think there should be a complete separation between literature and dishwashing."

—Flannery O'Connor

"You are marrying a writer. You must not expect her to do the dishes."

—Eleanor Ross Taylor

"I once was asked to tell one of my stories in my own words."

—Eudora Welty

INTRODUCTION

The essays in this book merge "life" and "literature." The first essay explains why. It is only by living that we learn what we need to know to write—and, also, to judge what we (and others) have written.

Is there any life that does not reenact the poems and stories that are a part of our communal consciousness? Or literature that does not show us how we might live in the world?

In writing these pieces, I chose to break one of the conventions of criticism, the one that says to keep separate the life and the work. The conventions of criticism, any kind of criticism, while useful for many purposes (helping us to grasp structure, theme, context, and subtext, but perhaps also encouraging us to replace the poem or story with our ideas about the poem or story), are necessarily limited, cannot take into account the entire transaction a specific text makes with a specific reader. Conventions are general, book and reader individual cases.

Here, then, are essays about writing and reading, especially but not exclusively reading women writers, that view life and literature as inherently and fortuitously intermingled, at the same time as they seek to understand the connections between the two.

I have ordered the essays in Part II to reflect, loosely, the chronology of my own life. "Authority," which, according to chronology, would appear later, constitutes Part I, with its overview of my life both in and out of literature. (This piece asserts my belief that many if not all of the decisions a writer makes at her desk are intimately bound to issues of personal and political morality.) Part III, "Called to It," is a short autobiography that supplies background for Part I. In general, my subject of inquiry in Part II is women writers, including myself: how we write and how we integrate writing, income-producing work (usually not writing), family, community, and self. In our culture, it seems impossible that a woman writer would remain unconscious of the semantic tension between the words *woman* and *writer*. To be a woman writer in our time is to ask what it *means* to be one.

"The Globe and the Brain: On Place in Fiction" includes several excerpts from my own work because I was asked to present a "lecture/reading." One essay is a crazy quilt patched together by sewing reviews to one another. One essay incorporates one short review into its aims. The remainder of the essays are whole pieces of cloth. Among the more personal pieces I have included critical essays about a few of the southern prose writers who have made an impression on me. Anne Tyler's novel *Saint Maybe* raises questions about good and evil, or right and wrong, that can never be answered but are infinitely interesting. Mary Ward Brown is still writing in her nineties, a model of dedication one hopes to emulate; her stories, to my mind, fill a gap in southern literature, reflecting, and reflecting upon, black-white relations in the fifties and sixties. Elizabeth Hardwick possessed a notably fine critical intelligence as well as a knack for incisive social observation. To some extent, as a young writer I daydreamed about occupying a position similar to hers in the literary world (writing for *The New York Review of Books*, hobnobbing with Serious Names); that she was a southerner made this daydream at least a tiny bit more realistic, although I'm now quite happy on a small farm far, far away. Bobbie Ann Mason's memoir about her hardscrabble background, and especially about her mother, moved me. My own family had been poor, but not nearly so poor as was hers.

Eudora Welty came to the University of North Carolina at Greensboro to give a reading when I was a writing student there; later, in 1995, I had the pleasure and honor of sitting beside her at a luncheon organized for her visit to Rhodes College in Memphis, where I was teaching for a semester. She had the loveliest voice, a soft, low, Mississippi drawl, and wore what looked like slippers, something I foresee myself doing in a few more years. One story of hers in particular has been a touchstone for me: "A Still Moment," with its comprehensive philosophical reach (and suspenseful plot).

Though no southerner, Grace Paley wrote stories I have read and reread. I was introduced to Cynthia Ozick in the offices of a Judaica publishing house, where I was working while writing the first draft of my first novel. She was kind and encouraging to a writer just starting out.

There are other women writers with whom I feel somehow connected or allied. Some I hope to write about. Some I imagine I'll never, alas, get to. It will still be a long while before the term *woman writer* becomes unuseful—I do hope someday it will be exactly that—and in the meanwhile women writers may look to one another for support, guidance, and a sense of the possibilities, if only by reading one another's work.

I

AUTHORITY

My old college friend, whom I had not encountered in twenty-five years, laughed, reminiscing about how young we'd been. How intense. How ready to call the world to account. "And *you*," he said. "You wouldn't give anyone an inch. Not a millimeter. You had the highest standards, and you wouldn't budge them for anybody."

Now, this was not the way I remembered myself. I remembered myself as shy. And eager to do the right thing. And sweet. Essentially, anyway. Essentially sweet! Beneath what—it was coming back to me now—could only be called an intellectual pugnaciousness. . . .

But I'd been so hesitant! I said. So aware that things looked at from one point of view could take on a different cast looked at from another! Not to mention so downright timid! (This is the way old friends renewing an acquaintance dwell on themselves, amazed to find that their lives have not moved through time so much as time has moved through their lives, uprooting expectations, overturning plans.) Had I really been so positive of my opinions?

Indeed, yes, he said.

And he was right. But even as we sat there over drinks and dinner in the restaurant with its huge windows that looked out on the mall, I still secretly believed that, if I had been an opinionated young person, I had been a very sweet opinionated young person.

∾:∾

Hindsight is one thing. In those earlier days, I was so accustomed to thinking of myself as fearful (even, for example, as I took my seat on the train for Moscow; or even as I put out the fire that a stoned roommate had started; or even as I quit my job to write) that the quality I was most mesmerized by in other writers' work, especially other women writers' work, was their conviction of their own authority. Whenever I read a woman who wrote with authority I was bowled over, I was prostrate with admiration. Some of these women writers—come to think of it, maybe all—were younger than I was, as if they had received as a birthright a sense of self that I was still struggling to achieve. I read their work again and again, trying to locate their sense of sureness. I found it in one writer's verbs, and in another's linguistic playfulness. Once I found it in a writer's omissions— the way she dared to leave certain information out of her poems.

It was easier, for me, to write poetry and fiction with authority than to write nonfiction with authority. Writing poetry or fiction, the writer creates her own world: coherence is one of her tasks, and more or less frequently verisimilitude may be another, but she need not worry whether any statement she makes within the work is true or false outside the work, not *really*. She achieves authority by being in control of her techniques (and her verbs, her linguistic playfulness, the knowledge of when it is effective to leave out something that might have been put in). She achieves a larger authority as she acquires scope—tonal, thematic, any kind of scope. She acquires scope one sentence at a time, one line at a time. She acquires it as she comes to know herself and the world she lives in. "Write an autobiography," a teacher, the fiction writer Ivan Gold, said, giving our class an assignment meant to bring the students closer, enhance the feeling of a literary community. I worked on mine all semester. At the end of the semester, it was four pages long. I felt that I knew nothing about myself and the world I lived in, or at least nothing that I could tell.

A shadow of secrecy darkened what I did know about my world. As bold as I might be about other things, there was a history that I did not dare approach, for fear of whom I might hurt. Perhaps this is why I thought of myself as fearful—even, for example, as I went to the cemetery in Riga at midnight in January 1965, during the Cold War, or—this was years later, in the States—exacted an apology from a hospital for assault. (I met with management in a rarely used conference room.)

I'm not going to reveal that secret here, because it's not necessary to know it in order to pursue the problem of authority in art. It's not even necessary to know why I met with management to exact an apology from the hospital....

It may be necessary, though, to know that there are traumas that rob the self of its belief in its ability to perceive accurately anything about itself or the world. This self navigates its days by a kind of negation: if something seems to be so, it must be not so. If something seems one way, it must be, in fact, another way. The self's own thoughts and feelings are presumed not to be what it thinks or feels they are. The syntax of such a self may grow exceedingly subtle in its search for a definition, having an ever increasing complexity to encompass, but subtlety is not authority, or not yet—not until it reaches into every aspect, and not until it can test its idea of itself in the world.

Subtle selves love the abstract. Like hiding an object in the open, subtlety covers itself in logic, in argument. I loved the process of creating a problem, of developing a line of thought whether theoretically or metaphorically. I was surprised to discover how few writers even attempt sustained argument or the creation of a new aesthetic problem. Sometimes I even thought that maybe they were incapable of doing these things, but now I think that they didn't need to do them: they were not in hiding, they could declare themselves, they could be, and were, visible, their words a reflection of personality. That is, they had a kind of authority.

In 1974 I published my first novel—in which the narrator puts out a fire that has been started by her stoned roommate. When *The Chicago Tribune* followed up a review of my novel by calling to ask if I would write a review of John Gardner's recent collection of short fiction, I blurted, utterly unprofessionally, "Do you think I can *do* it?"

As soon as I hung up the phone I began to think I was in over my head. I did! Because I thought that if one were going to voice one's opinions in *The Chicago Tribune*, they had better be *right*. If they were wrong, I thought, their wrongness would be added to the tally of critical wrongness that kept mounting over the centuries; I was afraid of being responsible for even a fraction of that tally. It had not yet occurred to me that one might change one's opinion.

It also did not occur to me that I could say no to reviewing a given book or request a specific book to review. I assumed it was my job to review whatever was sent to me for review. I think I assumed it was a type of homework.

In her posthumously published *Intellectual Memoirs* Mary McCarthy remembers writing book reviews for *The Nation* and *The New Republic* when she was barely into her twenties, and soon after that for *The Partisan Review*. My god, I think, reading this: she had writers' lives in her hands and she had not yet even written a book of her own. "I was rough," she confesses, with a dismay that strikes me as pro forma. "I laid about me right and left." She did not lack for a sense of authority. . . .

On the other hand, W. H. Auden told *The Paris Review* in 1974, "Writing nasty reviews can be fun, but I don't think the practice is very good for the character."

As I say, extending a line of thought as far as it could go without breaking in two exhilarated me, seemed the most exciting thing anyone could do with her life, but cutting the line short— stopping it here and there to say "And that's what I think about this" or "This is what I think about that"—seemed as drastic as castration. Maybe I *wouldn't* think that about this or this about that if I could just think things through. But reviewing was not about thinking things through; it was about having opinions. Or rather—this was the rub—it was about not only having them but going on record with them. But I hadn't wanted to disappoint *The Tribune's* book editor—that female trait, I assumed until recently, of being afraid to say no, as if book editors, like dates in high school, might fall ill with "blue balls" if one said no to them—and so I said yes and was now expected to write a review.

Recently I read Karl Shapiro's essay "What Is Not Poetry?" in which he recounts his first experience of reviewing. He had successfully submitted some poems to *Poetry*: "Immediately upon acceptance of the poems, the editor asked if I would undertake to write a review. Thinking it some kind of obligation or perhaps *honor* I accepted. . . .From then on I took it for granted that I was expected to write essays or reviews when asked, and I almost never refused." So maybe it is not just women who are inclined to be meekly accepting of tasks; maybe it is poets. Or maybe it was just Karl Shapiro and I. In any case, I was now expected to form an opinion—and propound it. I was about to become an authority.

Which is not at all like being an author.

What is it like to be an author in America? In his essay "The Age of Criticism" Randall Jarrell reports: "A novelist, a friend of mine, one year went to a Writers' Conference; all the other teachers were critics, and each teacher had to give a formal public lecture. My friend went to the critics' lectures, but the critics didn't go to his; he wasn't surprised; as he said, 'You could tell they knew I wasn't really literary like them.' "

Aware that I was "only" a writer, I remained diffident about my reviewing, and then about my essay-reviews and literary essays.

And yet each book I reviewed was a wonderful occasion for considering what I thought of it. And every opinion I arrived at required consideration in the light of my other opinions, which,

I began to see, one might change, one might have to change, one might enlarge one's view of the world by changing. . .

To review a book, I decided, required that I try to set aside my awareness of how I might have written it and participate in the book as the author had written it. It required that I analyze the book in the terms the book had set for itself. In a sense, then, in order to arrive at my opinion of the book I had first to relinquish any authority over it.

What an interesting process this was! The less a priori authority I claimed, the more authoritative I felt by the end of the book. This is diametrically opposed to what ideologues do: those people who read books through lenses provided by Freud, Marx, Derrida supply their lack of authority by assuming someone else's. But what does it mean "to participate in the book as the author had written it"?

Ideologues "all come different speaking" (to steal, from myself, a phrase on which, when I was twenty, I'd built a poem celebrating Wallace Stevens), but they all say the same thing. Feminists or Marxists or deconstructionists, they say that the poem or story or novel is what it is because it never could have been otherwise. Either the author was obliged to make the decisions she did and, furthermore, made them unwittingly, because history and her relation to it mandated those decisions, the text being constructed not by her but by psychological or social dynamics that she is too much a part of to perceive (though the critic of contemporary literature apparently retains a miraculous distance from said dynamics and so perceives everything, though not, unfortunately, quite enough to write a novel or a poem) or the author was never more than an accident of birth anyway, something like an appendix or sixth finger, that can be removed by a simple critical operation without injury to the text. The text remains whatever it is, which is what it was always going to be, though precisely what that is we do not know except as critics tell us. And what is that? Jarrell says, "An *Encyclopedia of Pseudo-Sciences* might define critical method as *the systematic (q.v.) application of foreign substances to literature; any series of*

*devices by which critics may treat different works of art as much alike
as possible."*

Given these constraints on a writer's ability to make
judgments, it was possibly not a bad thing that I hesitated to
make them. For years, I kept quiet.
(Even as I was, I now reveal, kicked out of several schools.
But I *did* my homework! And when my husband kicked me out
of marriage. I cried a bit, then, sitting on the bed as he yanked
clothes from the closet and slammed them into my suitcase. Later,
I did write a novel about a young couple whose marriage ends in
divorce—a comic novel, reversing the traditional definition of a
comic novel as one that ends with a marriage. It addressed the
question of free will versus determinism, as did Goethe's *Elective
Affinities.* And I was certainly somewhat less than quiet when I
badgered the Soviet consulate for a visa and fired off letters to
world leaders to urge support for the Helsinki Accords.)

Events take place, even in writers' lives. Of course, in
writers' lives the events that take place are sometimes writerly
events. To describe three such events: Writing, and, especially,
writing reviews, I began to think that from time to time a greater
authority may be secured by sacrificing a sprightly Strunk-and-
White verb in favor of a bald form of the verb "to be": placing
sentences in copulative relation can clarify clausal connection,
priority, and hierarchy (that is, valuation). I saw that linguistic
play can be a distraction, fascinating as light on water but not
a way to see to the depths. I saw that leaving things out can
produce a sophisticated surface that, ultimately, dies of lack
of intellectual and emotional nourishment, slickness a kind of
sickness. How much better to run the Tolstoyan risk of saying
too much, for the opposite danger is the glib, gestural story, the
glib, gestural poem.

(There were also events that were not writerly events. There
were deaths of people one loved, for example. Among them was
my ex-husband. He had been a sculptor, his artworks emblematic
of intellectual rigor as a source of beauty even in despair.)

In story or poem, as with reviewing, a certain submission
to the text takes place. T. S. Eliot argued that "[t]he emotion of

art is impersonal. And the poet cannot reach this impersonality without surrendering himself wholly to the work to be done." But, he suggested, the poet cannot surrender himself without a comprehensive knowledge of what he is surrendering to—the tradition. In other words, he cannot give himself over to what he has incompletely imagined, because where what is imagined remains incomplete that blankness will be filled in by *an idea of himself.* That is my phrase, not Eliot's. And by it is meant the opposite of what Yeats meant when he wrote that "even when the poet seems most himself, when he is Raleigh and gives potentates the lie, or Shelley 'a nerve o'er which do creep the else unfelt oppressions of this earth,' or Byron when 'the soul wears out the breast' as 'the sword outwears its sheath,' he is never the bundle of accident and incoherence that sits down to breakfast; he has been reborn as an idea, something intended, complete." To be reborn as an idea requires, first of all, shedding the idea of oneself. To become an intention is to be completed, imagined; it is, then, to be *created,* and the creation stands outside the creator.

The created work—the completely imagined work—can never be the poet's idea of herself. So much less can it be the critic's idea of the work. It is the realized idea of itself, which was accomplished by the author's ability to surrender herself to the text.

I think I'd better explain something here. A writer surrendering to a text is performing an act of love, but precisely because it is not self-love, it is an act that acquires authority as it acquires knowledge. This is why Eliot is correct to point to the living tradition, even if his own idea of the tradition may have been truncated by his privileged position in life. This is also why critics who like to think the text is caused by something other than an author show that they have only an elementary understanding of the creative process. The writer can give herself over to the text only by being conscious, at every moment, of the text and of the possibilities of the text. She reads the page as she writes it. That is the reading that transcends all critical readings. She reads what the page has to say to her, and she responds attentively, and the page responds, and in this dialogue is the creation, as if the Logos were to demand of us an answer to itself.

And does it not?

Robert Frost's essay "The Figure a Poem Makes" comes as close as anything to explaining this process. Wondering "how a poem can have wildness and at the same time a subject that shall be fulfilled," he states, "It should be of the pleasure of a poem itself to tell how it can." And then those well-known, true lines about the figure made by a poem, any poem: "It begins in delight, it inclines to the impulse, it assumes direction with the first line laid down, it runs a course of lucky events, and ends in a clarification of life—not necessarily a great clarification, such as sects and cults are founded on, but in a momentary stay against confusion."

The writer makes a mark on the page—a word, two words, a line, a sentence. She reads what she has written (what she has actually written, not what she has thought; this is difficult to do), and she responds to it with another word, or two words, another line, another sentence. And so it goes, a chancy thing at best but a terrifically conscious thing, a thing that insists on such concentration as must exclude any thought of the writer herself. Where is she in all this? She is lost, lost to the world, involved in an activity as risky as running rapids. If she keeps her balance, she ends with the poem, or the story or the novel, in a place of tranquility.

(One reason my husband had sent me packing was that I was ready to have a child, and he had decided that he did not want children. He must have worried that he couldn't trust me. Later, doctors told me I couldn't have children. Later still, I had a miscarriage. Then I applied for artificial insemination, but the university hospital refused to do the procedure because I was single. The married, male doctor looked me in the eye and dared to say this, despite funding from the state legislature. In order to transfer my medical coverage to a place that didn't discriminate against single women, I had to threaten to sue the hospital. This was not the same hospital where I had been assaulted and met with management. So many men in so many offices control women's lives. Do you think this is no longer the case?)

The poet, like a woman who wants to conceive a child, believes in what she is doing. She possesses this faith, a faith in the thing to be done, that carries her past boulders, over the undertow, downstream. She has always had this faith, even when she did not always have faith in her ability to do the thing. This is how it is that she sometimes does what she thought she could not do. She may even write and publish an autobiography.

This autobiography may begin with a young woman—a sweet young woman!—stepping onto a train bound for Moscow, the doors between cars shuttered with sheets of ice. The "thaw" of Khrushchev's rule was over. . .

While giving herself up to her work, she has learned— parenthetically, as if in a kind of amplification of the narrative that is she—something about herself and the world she lives in.

Camus argued that "great style is not a mere formal virtue. It is a mere formal virtue when it is sought out for its own sake to the detriment of reality, but then it is not great style. It no longer invents, but imitates—like all academic works—while real creation is, in its own fashion, revolutionary." Camus insisted that an essential difference between art and criticism is that art is a revolutionary act. In his book-length meditation *The Rebel*, he explains that revolution is possible only in a civilized society. A society *centralized* by tyranny, either of ideology or production—that is, I would say, a society in which there are no *citizens*—cannot provide the freedom necessary for hope, and hope is another word for revolution. "Language destroyed by irrational negation becomes lost in verbal delirium; subject to determinist ideology, it is summed up in the slogan. Halfway between the two lies art."

Almost forty years after the publication of *The Rebel*, Soviet Communism dwells in the ruined halls of its own vicious history, the ghost of millions of vanished, torn lives. But can the United States stop pontificating about "family values" long enough to create a civilized society, or are we already in decline, in bitter thrall to "the drama of our times in which work, entirely subordinated to production, has ceased to be creative"? A society in which the government's annual budget for military bands enormously outspends that for the arts is a society perilously unconcerned with civilizing itself. Is it so mild a business to civilize oneself? Camus speaks of "the generosity of rebellion, which unhesitatingly gives the strength of its love and without a moment's delay refuses injustice." That is also the generosity of art: to confer itself on the world. Needing to do this, it emerges from hiding, it shows its face. With "a burning humility" it finds its voice to speak for a people, an age.

Art has defined itself, though Camus does not say this, by its rebellion, first of all, against the formlessness of what it used to be. A great oppression, felt in the nerves, attempted to deny to art the freedom to formulate itself, but oppression depends on secrecy, and art has rebelled against secrecy and formlessness. In that formlessness it saw death and the totalitarianism of time. It confronted death and seized meaning from time's armed thugs, which until then had seemed overwhelmingly powerful. It did this, first of all, by living.

Criticism, too, must be alive, if it is to mean anything at all. "We become good critics," Jarrell avowed, "by reading poems and stories and by living." To any critic who doubts this, what can a writer say except "get a life"?

II

I used to be a gang-leader.

This was in the third grade, in Ithaca, New York, a place as mythical in my consciousness now as his own home must have seemed to Odysseus, wandering so long and far. My family had moved there from the Deep South when I was four; we moved back south when I was nine: five years that are like a long dream of snow, a time out of mind.

The kids in my gang were boys. There was another gang, made up of girls, led by Patty, Queen of the Garbage Cans.

Soon after our arrival in the frozen north, my parents realized they had made a mistake. They had naively assumed that life north of the Mason-Dixon Line would be more serious, more successful, than life in the frivolous south. I know what they thought, for their disappointment was like a clarifying flame, after which the hopes that had brought them there were a hard, clear residue, recognizable by us all, bitter to taste. It was not possible to look back and say, Well, but we never really intended for things to be different! *They had intended for things to be different.* They had thought that a glow of cultural sophistication would overlay life in the north, like a sheen on the snow, like the glow from the Aurora Borealis, which I saw once. My parents were the kind of people who always imagine that things will be "better" elsewhere—more exciting, less frustrating. My father, especially, having been born into a once-well-to-do family that was by his time grim with poverty, brought north with him like the dead weight of an albatross a dysfunctional nostalgia for an image of intellectual glamor that would be hard to realize anywhere in modern America. He craved a life of the mind.

It wasn't there for him in Ithaca. In Ithaca, my father taught a killing schedule and, at night, practiced the violin or rehearsed string quartets. To add to their miniscule income, my mother typed dissertations for Cornell students or menus for the diner across the street, all day and half the night. She also practiced the violin and rehearsed string quartets. She played second fiddle to my father's first (but only where string quartets were concerned). Often they had evening quartet performances. Often they were gone from the apartment.

They were determined people, my parents. They never stopped working. When my mother received the news, from Gulfport, Mississippi, that her beloved father had died, she typed "for thirty-six hours straight, just as if my heart had not been permanently broken." Both my mother and my father were much too busy—and worried, unhappy, and distracted—to pay much attention to my siblings and me. We children lived our own lives. Anything we did was fine, as long as we stayed out from "underfoot."

All this activity took place in a railroad flat three flights above a grocery store, on College Avenue. I'm given to understand that this is now a desirable neighborhood, gentrified; then, it was a downtown street crowded with tenements, separated from the Cornell campus by Suicide Bridge—so called because flunking students were said to leap from it in their shame—and by a snobbish disregard that had cast the city, so far as the campus was concerned, well beyond the pale.

On rainy days, I sat under the awning of Tony's Barber Shop, scraping the dye from bottle tops I was allowed to gather from his Coke machine. Hour after hour, I scraped those bottle tops, until I had hundreds of shiny, silver "coins"—though that metaphor is an afterthought, and in fact, I can't imagine why I did this, or what I did with them. I suppose I just liked sitting under Tony's awning and scraping bottle tops until they were silver. When the weather was warm, I went roller-skating, or explored the gorge.

Cascadilla Gorge, as I remember it—and this is, after all, myth I'm talking about here, not journalism—is a deep-sided elevator into time. I could yell war-whoops and those high cliffs would give them back to me in the shouts of Indians chanting and dancing around a bright fire, the paint on their glare-stricken faces as red as wounds, as yellow as scars, as black as death.

Or I could go further back, and further, into the time of King Kong. There were gorillas in the gorge and spiny, prehistoric fish in the deep, secretive pools.

When it snowed—and I remember Ithaca as mostly lost in snow—my big brother sledded down Tower Hill, but my kid sister and I took our sled to the little slope next to the Triangle Book Store, across the street from our building and down the street from the diner. I remember a prized day with my scarce father when he pushed my sister and me down that miniature—but how big to us—rise, then pulled us up, then pushed us down again, and how snow got packed in our mittens and we'd lick at it and then have to take our mittens off to pick the wool fibers out of our curious, always curious, mouths.

But my parents were depressed, angry, frenetic. They couldn't get used to the low-ceilinged skies. They thought Yankees were humorless, a strange breed of people with minds as dull as the sunless days. For twenty cents a page, plus two cents a carbon, my mother typed a ridiculous Ph.D. dissertation about kissing habits.

(But she fell in love with the freshman from Pakistan who wrote a history paper extolling Disraeli as "England's utmost statesman.")

What had she done, she wondered, to deserve a life of typing term papers on T. S. Eliot and, for stupid graduate students, theses, scrubbing laundry in the bathtub on a washboard, married to a man who didn't even like to go dancing, if they could have afforded it? And to think that when he'd finally turned up at her parents' house in Gulfport, in a Buick he'd bought for seventy-five dollars at a bankruptcy sale, she was already booked for dates for the whole week, one night after the other, each with a different boy, and she had had to get her mother to call each of them up and cancel the engagements with the excuse that her daughter was "sick"! Of course, my father in his new Buick was handsome, and smart and, by Gulfport standards, sophisticated, but my mother hated the cold. She hated being stuck in that monstrously monotonous apartment. She would have liked to go dancing.

We the children began to get into trouble. My brother was caught joyriding in a stolen car. My sister got her forehead split open by a baseball bat one recess.

And I was the leader of a gang. And proud to have the boys in my class in my gang, while Patty was stuck with girls and, famously, garbage cans. (*Why did we say that? What on earth could we have meant by that?*)

All the gang members had jackknives. Mine was a smooth, dark blue. We threw hard-packed snowballs at one another, and other gangs would sometimes build a snowball around a stone. One day Patty was cruel to my kid sister and I grabbed her glasses right off her nasty, pale face and threw them on the ground (but made sure they'd land safely on the grass). While she was down on her knees feeling blindly for them, I grabbed my sister's hand and raced with her to the end of the block. Then, a seven-year-old hero, I detoured my sister through the Triangle Book Store, where Patty would never think to look for us even if she did find her glasses. We would double back down College Avenue toward home.

Just as we emerged from the store, Patty sprang out of no-where and pushed me off my feet. I was pinned to the sidewalk, staring straight into her furious face.

She banged the back of my head against the cement pavement. Again and again, she did this. No one stopped her; this was street life in our neighborhood. I once saw a boy chase a girl into the street with a knife. I once put out a fire a boy started in the alley next to my building. My sister erupted into tears and ran home for help.

I did not cry. Not then or when I got shots or when the principal, Mrs. Fawcett, whom we nicknamed, pleased with our cleverness, Old Lady Drip, called me into her office, or when I had to stay after school. Not when the goldfish died or when my birthday present was a Hershey bar or when the woman downstairs, without asking me or my mother if this was what I wanted, cut off my waist-length dark-brown hair, or when my eardrum burst and pus poured out all over the pillow and I knew I couldn't interrupt a rehearsal so I waited until the violist and cellist had gone home before I got out of bed to tell my parents, and not even when *my* forehead was split open, by a piece of glass pitched in a battle between two small armies of bigger-than-me boys and I had to have stitches without anesthesia in a retired doctor's apartment because the hospital was too far away. But I almost cried when we were told we would be leaving Ithaca, because I knew it meant I would never own the holster set in Woolworth's window.

Two bright-silver pistols in a holster lined with green felt: I thought they were beautiful. My parents thought they were unnecessary. That was because they didn't understand what they were necessary for—to complete my outfit as The Phantom. I planned to ride a wild black stallion along the tops of high, pointed ridges in forlorn and dangerous country. In the daytime, my white trousers and white shirt and white boots, silver six-guns and silver spurs would be set off by a white cape; at night when I had important missions to carry out, I would reverse the cape to its black otherside, and on my black horse I would disappear into the dark, invisible but on the side of the law.

From the back window of the old Kaiser that replaced the old Buick, I gazed at Woolworth's like, I think, a lover obliged to renounce happiness for the sake of a nobler ideal. At last we were on our way, and I turned back around and got out my spiral notebook and began to write in it "I will be good" one hundred times, as my teacher had told me to do. I don't think it occurred to me to write anything else.

My brother looked at the page. Our sister was squeezed between us in the back seat. "You are never going back to East Hill Elementary," he said to me over her head, "so why bother doing that?"

Did he think I was a dummy? I knew I was never going back to East Hill. But why *was* I filling up the page with words? It must have been like hanging around at Tony's. I suppose I just liked writing a sentence in a spiral notebook the same way I liked scraping bottle tops.

Maybe I was intrigued by the process of transforming something: making a bottle top an *objét* whose wordless beauty was all that mattered; filling a blank page until it became something else, if only a filled page.

Maybe I enjoyed concentrating on almost anything because it lifted me out of time, which, already, was otherwise oppressive and overwhelming.

I ignored my brother and kept writing.

I don't really know why.

I WAS A TEENAGE BEATNIK

I was eighteen and attending the University of Tennessee at Knoxville. "Attending" may be too strong a word. I was more often absent from than present in my classes, which included nuclear physics and symbolic logic, both of which I was flunking. In nuclear physics students perched high on bleachers and stared down at the Oak Ridge scientist on the stage, whose accent was untranslatable to my ears. The symbolic logic professor had a floating eye and bounced on sponge-soled shoes in front of the room. In my literature class, and I believe I must have been flunking that class, too, we were reading *Don Quixote* and James Joyce's *Ulysses*, both of which were over my junior-year head, although I kept trying to get through *Don Quixote*, because it was one of my father's two favorite books. (The other was *Tom Jones*.) The Modern Library edition lay on the table in the single back room I rented in a boarding house, and each day I read some of it. But everything was over my head that semester. It wasn't only literature and logic and physics I couldn't grasp; I didn't know who I was or why everything I did turned out such a mess and made my parents angry. I didn't know why the school nurse had sent me to the school psychiatrist or why the psychiatrist said my answers to his Rorschach test meant I had "a male mind in a female body." I was completely mystified about my female body, which at least one graduate student, an Alpha Male from Memphis named Curly Matthews, hijacked to a mountain cabin, there, with the tacit encouragement of friends, to seduce me, except that I sat up all night with my back against the headboard, chewing my nails to the quick and supplying arguments drawn from symbolic logic as to why I should not lose my virginity to him.

What the hell was stately, plump Buck Mulligan yakking about, anyhow? If he was going to shave, why didn't he just shut up and shave? What was so amusing about young men behaving pretentiously, showing off their recently acquired knowledge and wanting everyone to admire their wit? The towertop, Babel-onian dialogue between Mulligan and Stephen Dedalus was so arch and so cluttered with signposts directed toward the reader (Don't miss any of these neat allusions to Christian theology and classical mythology! They're here to tip you off! Think Greek!) that I immediately felt wary, hostile, defensive. The author had no intention of leading the reader on a journey into the unknown; like his characters, he just wanted to show off.

At the same time, Joyce's dancing words dizzied me with their dazzle. When I endeavored to imagine the view from the tower, I felt as if I were falling right over the stone railing. Try as I might, I couldn't see it, "the scrotumtightening sea." I just didn't know what that was. Literature is supposed to expand the imagination, beyond gender as well as other barriers, but I seemed to have trouble conjuring an imaginary world, at any rate while the real one at hand was so unaccountable and strange.

A classmate came to my rented room to talk about writing. We exchanged manuscripts and were offering each other a critique when the landlady's brother burst into the room without knocking and kicked the boy out. The man then turned to me and told me, not so nicely as this, that I would have to move. I moved to an apartment so endowed with cockroaches I did not dare sleep or undress in it. Cockroaches could crawl all over me, my female body. My male mind cringed at this thought, perhaps effeminately. The formerly-a-closet shower, with a sheet hung from tacks on the side where the door used to be, was in the living room and served as a kind of nest or meeting room for the cockroaches. I showered in the gym at the university instead. No wonder, then, that when I went to my classes, I slept through them. I was taking three other classes, and I don't even remember what they were. And those were the ones in which I got A's.

I met people. We congregated in the student union. Someone gave me a copy of *The Well of Loneliness* to read. (My sexuality seemed to be on a lot of people's minds, but I would have been happy just to get through a book, any book.) Another acquaintance spoke vaguely of how a guy named Cruiser had gone to Mexico and brought back "stuff." Well, I did say "those days." This was so long ago, longer than anyone then could have predicted it would be now. The previous summer I had ridden the bus from Richmond to Knoxville, stayed at the YWCA, and searched for a room to rent and in my high heels and pink-and-white polkadot sundress I had felt summery and excited, but already, during registration, I was bewildered, confused, afraid, and now I had lost the ability to read even books that had the advantage of not being class assignments. *The Well of Loneliness* was more eccentric, to me, than *Ulysses*, less sequential than *Don Quixote*, and I didn't have a clue. What I took away from *The Well of Loneliness* was a determination that whatever I wrote was not going to be murky.

I revealed to my new crowd my intention of being a writer, and the leader asked to see some of my poems. He was tall, dark, commanding, with an air of desperation about him; his wife had long blond hair and looked like Mary (the Mary then) of Peter, Paul, and Mary. I thought they were glamorously anti-bourgeois and I admired them fiercely, and looking back, I think they must have been kind people, because they encouraged me in my belief that I was meant to be a writer.

Another member of the group was a fellow I had met back in the summer on my scouting trip, who had written me letters when

I returned to Richmond. "I gather from your poetry," he wrote in one of them, "that you are no stranger to the sheets." Wanting not to be murky, I had been imaginatively explicit where, I now realized, murk might have been preferable. I was ashamed to tell him the truth so I let him think he was right, but when I showed a poem to my mother, over Christmas break, in which I used the word *nipple*, she had what the doctor explained to us was a "mock heart-attack" and went to bed in her attic room and said she never wanted to see me again. My father was disgusted with me; he thought I had killed her, or more or less killed her, or at any rate sort of mock-killed her.

Whatever guys may have thought about their chances with me, they took to dropping by the apartment, in spite of the cockroaches. They'd come over and we'd sit around talking about books and art and ideas. Answering a knock on my door one night I threw open the door to find myself facing two cops. "There have been complaints," they said, "that you are entertaining men here at all hours. Men have been seen entering and leaving this apartment at all hours."

I was shocked. Could they really be thinking what they seemed to be implying? "I'm not a prostitute," I said, feelingly. "I'm a poet!"

They told me I would have to move.

Luckily, I had met a girl from Shady Valley, Tennessee, who was studying painting. She was the first in her family to go to college and seemed to know what she was doing in a way that I did not. We moved into an apartment together. It was clean and had no cockroaches. Every night people would come to our apartment to read poetry aloud while candles, burning in wine bottles, dripped wax down the glass sides, stratifying over the labels until it looked like a relief map—or the paint on a van Gogh canvas, the way it threatens the viewer, seems to want to reach out and embrace the viewer (to death maybe), pull the viewer into the painting. We read Ginsberg and Ferlinghetti. I read *A Coney Island of the Mind* and managed to understand it. Maybe I wasn't a hopeless case. I read Céline's *Journey to the End of the Night* and *The Journal of Albion Moonlight* by Kenneth

Patchen and Jean Toomer's *Cane* and understood them. Maybe I could even become a hopeful case. We drank the wine before we turned the bottles into makeshift candlesticks, but no one had any "stuff." One of the women kept having to fly to Cuba for, she said, abortions; the way I remember it, she had about three in the space of two weeks. Her boyfriend was Cuban. I say "one of the women," but most of our guests, like mine of the previous month, were guys, and if anyone else besides the Cuban was having sex I didn't know about it. Mainly, we let our brains and tongues grow a little fuzzy with rotgut-red, aspired to the world-weariness of Jelly Roll Morton or Jean Genet or Christopher Isherwood, stayed up too late, and, more and more, skipped classes. Except Maline; coming from Shady Valley, she knew better than to skip class.

In Virginia, my parents were building a house; they were often at the site, where there was as yet no telephone. The dean called me in to his office to inform me that he had spoken with my father at the school where he taught. "He said you used to play the piano," the dean said, as if pleasantly chatting.

"Yes," I said. "I quit because I decided to be a writer instead."

"Your father said you quit because you had no talent."

I left his office reeling with his punches but unable to get in touch with my father. I didn't know how to call my father at work and didn't think he would have liked for me to.

The next time the dean called me in, he said, "There have been reports that you have been seen riding on the back of a motorcycle."

"I've never been on a motorcycle," I said, truthfully.

"That's not what the reports say."

What reports? Whose reports? Why would anyone give a damn whether I was on the back of a motorcycle?

Did I mention that I was finding this world unaccountable and strange?

The dean summoned Maline, too, but she simply let him say whatever he wanted to say and then went on doing what she was doing (and she was still attending her classes).

I fell a little bit in love with a boy who had dropped out or already finished or never had been in college; I didn't seem to know exactly what his status was, but he was an artist, a painter, and kept late hours, appearing and disappearing as if, unlike the rest of us, he had things to do besides just sit around in diners listening to country music on the juke box and holding forth on art and literature. I was intrigued. I tried to get him to notice me, but he told me I was too young, unformed, "a bitty thing needing to be unhooked and thrown back into the sea." Rejected, I consoled myself with daily sundaes at the drugstore, putting on poundage, though since I weighed about ninety-two to begin with I was not in danger of becoming overweight, but I knew the drugstore clerk was concerned about my state of mind (he didn't know it was a male mind) and I avoided meeting his eyes when I ordered another sundae.

The dean kept badgering me. The phone would ring and it would be his secretary telling me that the dean would expect me in his office at such and such an hour, and I would know that when I went there he would tell me how disappointed in me my father was, how my father was so fed up he wasn't sure he even wanted to claim me as his daughter anymore. The dean said my father was going to stop sending me money for rent and food, and sure enough, no more money arrived. Maline and I shoplifted peanut butter and jelly and a loaf of bread from the local market, the kind of corner shop that still had a wooden floor and penny-slot vending containers, shaped like space helmets, for jawbreakers and gum. When someone played rhythm-and-blues on the phonograph I felt I knew rhythm, I felt I knew blues.

"Tell me about your friends," the dean said, "and maybe I can talk your father into sending you some money." He wanted to know about the guy from Cuba: what were his politics? why did his girlfriend fly to Cuba so frequently?

Now, how was I supposed to know the answer to that when I couldn't even read the Great Novels on the reading list for my lit course?

"I don't know," I said.

And, "I don't know," I said again.

I knew better than to mention the word *abortion*.

"Your father," the dean said, "is very unhappy to hear about your motorcycle riding."

The usual crowd was in Maline's and my apartment the night I received a telegram from my father. "COME HOME NOW STOP," it said. "WILL NOT PAY TUITION FOR NEXT SEMESTER STOP."

I showed the telegram to my current boyfriend—or friend; he was not quite a boyfriend, but he was gentle and caring and I liked him. This was not the moody, mysterious painter but a student who planned to go to law school. Stilton James read the telegram and then held it in the flame from the candle until it caught fire and crumpled into ash.

The next day I went to the registrar's office and officially dropped out. Then, in his office, the dean handed me a bus ticket to Richmond that my father had sent care of him.

The morning I was to leave, Stilts and I were in the apartment alone; he had come over to help me finish packing. Once, I happened to glance out a window, and there were two patrolmen—or state troopers, or campus guards, but definitely a pair, as before—and they were checking around the back of the building. They seemed to be looking for me. The bus wasn't due to leave for six or eight hours but the empty apartment was creepy, and the cops were creepy. Stilts and I were ready to go anyway, so while the cops were still out back we walked down the front steps, got in Stilts's car, and drove to the bus station, where we sat quietly at a little table behind a paperback rack, drank coffee, and occasionally murmured some small comment. A half hour before the bus pulled in, Stilts flipped through the paperback rack and picked out a book. He paid for the book and then handed it to me. "You'll need something to read on the bus," he said. It was *The Dharma Bums* by Jack Kerouac.

I said thank you, and then the bus came, and Stilts gave my suitcase to the driver to stow in the storage compartment, and I got on the bus and found a window seat and waved good-bye to my friend.

It was a long ride—fourteen or fifteen hours. I was too shy to strike up a conversation with anyone. I watched the scenery until the bus began to fill up with shadows, as if all the empty seats were being taken by ghosts, the shades of a Blue Ridge Elysium. Gears shifted as we climbed, we drove through a brief rainstorm, passengers sighed or mumbled or fished in their pockets or handbags for peanut butter-and-jelly sandwiches (as did I), but the bus seemed haunted by silence and darkness. When it was full night, I switched on the overhead light and read Kerouac.

Every so often I'd put the book down on the empty seat beside me. When, at twelve, I renounced the piano—it had been a renunciation, a public declaration of my dedication to writing—I was working on a Beethoven sonata. The only person who had complained about my lack of talent then was me. I didn't think I could be a *great* pianist. (Maline says now—after all these years, we wound up living a couple of blocks apart and, though no longer in Tennessee, still painting and still writing—"You didn't just tell us you wanted to be a writer. You said you were going to be a great writer." "I did?" I ask, disbelieving, wondering how I could have been so bold, so self-revealing, so, above all for a southerner, impolite.)

My parents met me at the bus station in Richmond but, I learned, they had gone there not expecting me and only because they didn't know what else to do. It seems the Tennessee dean had telephoned my father to say that I had disappeared. "An all-points bulletin has been issued," he informed my father. "We're sure we'll find her." While I was catching the bus, riding the bus, getting off the bus, police were combing the city, scouring the state. The dean told my parents he thought I might be hiding out in the hills, perhaps with a graduate student. Or, he said, I might have run off to San Francisco. It was quite likely, he said, that I had gotten knocked up and had run away to New York City and been chopped into small pieces by a back-alley surgeon who regularly botched his unholy manipulations. Some instinct brought my parents to the station anyway.

As relieved as my parents were to see me step off the bus, my mother was staring hard at my stomach, which was, because of all those hot fudge sundaes, rounder than before. Hardly a word was said on the way home, home being the old house I was used to. The next morning, my big brother came in to wake me; he'd been delegated the task of finding out what was going on with me. (He was often delegated this task.) He picked up *The Dharma Bums* from the chair where I had tossed it. "Aha," he said, "I thought so." I knew from that that everyone had already decided what was going on with me, so I said nothing. For weeks I said nothing, or nothing much. What did I have to say to a father who thought I was talentless? To a mother who cast a shrewd eye on my stomach whenever I wore anything not black and outsized? To a brother who nodded knowingly whenever I did wear something black and outsized?

My kid sister said she was ashamed of me.

My mother said, "Putting on a little weight around the middle, are we?"

I was not about to explain to her that she had nothing to worry about. *Let her worry*, I thought. *It serves her right.*

I thought if she had a problem because she thought I was pregnant, it was a problem she had created for herself.

After a while, of course, it became clear that I was not pregnant. I lost weight and became again my usual skinny self, although still wearing black turtleneck sweaters and white lipstick. Eventually we began to talk about what had happened. We discovered that the dean had been lying to both my parents and me. Why? Rumors that reached me suggested an involvement within the state of Tennessee with planning for operations in the Bay of Pigs (hence, the thinking went, the trips to Cuba). For my part, I supposed that the university wanted to break up a group of what they considered troublemakers—*Poets! Painters! They might as well be prostitutes!*—and realized I was the easiest student to go after first. Years later Maline told me she thought the university had not liked the fact that our group was integrated, and I now think that is the most plausible explanation. I was officially expelled. My parents moved into the new house, and I, unable to find a school willing to have me, moved with them. In my new room I began to write a novella. The pages piled up. It wasn't

Joyce or Cervantes, but neither of them had been himself at my age either. At least I understood what I was reading now. I was making things clear for myself.

What does a novelist or even a budding novella-writer seek to clarify? A question. (A great novelist confronts a great question.) The answer to the question is the unknown upon which the novelist, with the reader, advances (but does not necessarily arrive at or define). The novelist who already has the answer before beginning to write risks no transformation of self and offers the reader no opportunity for a transformation of self. It is the clarity of the question that counts, not the answer. It is the question, not the answer, that moves and involves and educates the reader. Obviously, this is not to suggest that a great question is *all* that is needed to make a great novelist.

I finished my novella, put it in a desk drawer, and began composing letters to colleges. Even now, it would not be easy to find one that would take me.

Meanwhile, the dean had kept after Maline, but she wasn't to be budged. She finished college and was accepted for graduate work in art at the University of Iowa. *After* she was at Iowa, she received a letter from the dean at the University of Tennessee in Knoxville saying she *would not be allowed to return there!*

As Maline says, *What a wuss.*

A few months later my parents, frantic with worry, had to call the Chesterfield County Volunteer Rescue Squad for help finding my sister and her longtime steady boyfriend, who were out past curfew. The Rescue Squad shone a flashlight on them in a room over a garage at the boyfriend's house. Reminded of her own walk on the wild side, my sister wrings the dishcloth dry, drapes it over the kitchen faucet, and laughs.

I did find a college to take me. The dean there had a daughter who had been kicked out of Swarthmore, so he felt a certain sympathy for my plight and went to bat for me. The year after I was a beatnik I completed a major in philosophy, wore shirtwaist dresses, kneesocks, and loafers, and got the modern dance instructor to promise me a B in return for sitting quietly in the bleachers, reading, and not wrecking class morale with my total inability to execute a single dance movement.

More time passed. I went to graduate school in philosophy. The Bay of Pigs was a fiasco, Dallas a disaster. Stilton James took a job in District Attorney Jim Garrison's office in New Orleans. Several of our group were drafted, including the intriguingly aloof artist. A second Kennedy was murdered. Martin Luther King, Jr., died by an assassin's bullet in Memphis. Cities burned. I read *Krapp's Last Tape* by Samuel Beckett, was in utter awe of it, bought a recording of it, and listened to it over and over. People gave parties for the Black Panthers. "Ah, Dedalus, the Greeks," Buck Mulligan had mused. "I must teach you. You must read them in the original." Now I took the words to heart and studied *The Iliad*, memorizing some of it. I married, divorced, lived in New York and England. I returned to *Ulysses*, got through it and was stunned by the beauty of Joyce's descriptions of the ordinary world. Mythology aside, linguistic games aside, a "mockturtle vapour and steam of newbaked jampuffs" pulled the reader into "Harrison's," outside which "[a] barefoot arab stood over the grating, breathing in the fumes. Deaden the gnaw of hunger that way. Pleasure or pain is it?" Father Conmee's ankles were "thinsocked" and "tickled by the stubble of Clongowes field." Molly recalled "the firtree cove a wild place I suppose it must be the highest rock in existence the galleries and casemates and those frightful rocks and Saint Michaels cave with the icicles or whatever they call them hanging down and ladders all the mud plotching my boots." In the "Ithaca" episode, Leopold Bloom carefully observed on the top of the stove "a blue enamelled saucepan" and "a black iron kettle." Joyce's odyssey through Dublin was navigated detail by detail. Perhaps the psychiatrist at the University of Tennessee in Knoxville would have said that Joyce had a female mind in a male body.

The Beats were followed by metafictioneers, ethnonovelists, minimalists, and the new maximalists. In 1983 Joyce Johnson published a finely tuned book titled *Minor Characters* in which she described her youthful love affair with Jack Kerouac. When she told Jack she was writing a novel, he asked her to name her favorite novelist. "I said Henry James, and he made a face, and said he figured I had all the wrong models, but maybe I could be a great writer anyway. He asked me if I rewrote a lot, and said you should never revise, never change anything, not even a word. . . .He was going to look at my work and show me that what you wrote first was always best. I said okay, feeling guilty for all that I'd rewritten, but I still loved Henry James."

I love Joyce Johnson.

Terrorists took to bombing and poisoning. Ireland's turmoil—like Yugoslavia's, Africa's, India's, the Mideast's—seemed eternal, but elsewhere the invasion of Grenada, the Persian Gulf War, the devastating fires in Indonesia came and went. Governments came and went—the Soviet Union went!—celebrities came and went. The world changed; it always does, of course, but when you are eighteen, you do not always believe it will. I changed, too. It was a short while a long time ago that I was a teenage beatnik, and I am sure that there is much about that time that I've forgotten, but I remember being kidnaped by Curly, shown the door of the boarding house, evicted by cops who thought I was a working girl, expelled by a devious, ditzy dean, abandoned by books, and dispraised by my parents.

I had thought such picaresque memories would compose a comic memoir. It's not as if I've never earned a laugh or two now and then, spinning them as conversational anecdotes. I have come to understand why my father treasured Cervantes and Fielding, and I would have liked to write a good-humored memoir of innocence-at-large. Or if not that, I thought, then something lyrical and lovely, something just a little bit Samuel Barberish, *Knoxville: Semester of 1959.* Where did all the sadness come from?

It is so interesting how something will appear on a page out of nowhere, or as if it's been hiding in a shadowy corner waiting for someone to walk into the room and turn on the light. I never knew this sadness was there.

But so what. I still spin my anecdotes in conversation, and they still get laughs. "I was a teenage beatnik," I say. "I was eighteen, a junior at the University of Tennessee."

THE BEAUTY MARK

My mother was beautiful, but she never gave much thought to this fact. She rarely bothered with makeup. She wore red lipstick, as did most women of her generation, and that was about it. Taking a quick look in the mirror on nights she had a concert to play, she rubbed rouge onto her cheeks. No mascara or eye shadow or foundation or powder; she didn't need them. In her tulle or satin evening gown, her bare shoulders perhaps protected by a net stole, she looked like Katharine Hepburn. She looked like Ingrid Bergman. She looked better than Ingrid Bergman and Katharine Hepburn put together.

People tell me, "Your mother was the most beautiful woman I ever saw."

But she was busy. She had violin parts to practice, plus a job, plus kids—and we were difficult kids, always in some kind of trouble—and not enough money to pay the bills.

She wasn't interested in her own beauty, but she was interested in mine. She wanted me to meet and marry somebody famous. She wanted me to get my picture in the paper. She hired a professional photographer. The photographer took me out into the woods, shot some film and promptly dropped his pants. I was twenty and sarcastic. I asked, "Is that the whole thing?" He put his pants back on.

My mother ran her department-store credit card up to the limit buying cocktail dresses for me, so I would have something to wear at the mixers I would go to after I'd been rushed by a sorority. One dress was French blue silk, a lovely, subtle color drifting on the spectrum somewhere between soft gray and the palest summer sky. Another was black lace with a fishtail flounce, slinky and dangerous. I even bought one myself, using weeks of allowance, a Kelly green, long-sleeved, tight-fitting jersey sheath. I must have forgotten for a moment who I was, myself or my mother, because this was throwing money away. I was a bookworm, wanting only to read, write, think. Oh, and talk ideas long into the night with a friend or two. I never went to any of the sorority rushes, never married anyone famous.

Besides, how could I in my cocktail dresses meet the standard set by my mother in her evening gowns? There was pretty; there was even beautiful; and then there was my mother. Next to my mother, beautiful became not good enough, became unbeautiful, became—there is no other word—ugly.

Some days I did not venture out-of-doors simply because I thought I should not be seen. When I did go out (always wearing foundation, powder, eye shadow, eye liner, mascara) and people called me beautiful, I thought they were trying to make me feel better. I always said a simple thank you, because it would have been bad manners to say anything else, but I never believed them. At the same time, I could look in a mirror and see that some girls had it worse. So I did not complain. I just hid.

I had saved some money—working a day job, a night job, and a weekend job—to go to Europe. I was going to live in a garret and write poems. I booked passage on a small freighter to Rotterdam, boarded a train for Amsterdam, found a garret. I wrote poems.

One day I noticed that I seemed to be gaining weight. This

was strange, because my frugal standard of living required me to, mostly, not eat. I ate crackers and liverwurst and the only thing I drank was water. The weight was all in one place: I was developing a double chin. It grew and grew and became huge. I had to wear a cowl sweater so I could pull the neck of it up to my chin.

It was January now, and cold, especially in the garret. I found a pub with a roaring fire next to a small round table where I would go and sit and write my poems. One night a Dutchman approached me. We chatted for a while. Then he said, "What a shame. You'd be beautiful, if it weren't for this." And he reached across the table and jiggled my double chin, because the sweater's neck had fallen down.

I moved to London, where I found a room in a house with other would-be writers, artists, actors. One day, feeling panicky, I asked my landlord if he knew a doctor. Soon I was having an operation in the Florence Nightingale Hospital for Gentlewomen.

Back in the States, I had several more operations over the following year for a cyst between the thyroid and the larynx. It is unusual for a thyroglossal cyst to return, but mine did, several times. After the last operation I was not allowed to see my face, which, apparently, had swollen to preposterous proportions. (At my mother's insistence, a nurse had removed the mirrors from the hospital room.) Still, after the swelling went down, I looked the same as I had precyst.

The doctor said I would not survive another operation and administered a series of X-ray treatments to stop the cyst from recurring. Not until I entered my forties did my face begin to seem to me slightly lopsided. It can't sag on the side that got the X-ray treatment, but, of course, does on the other side. I am fairly self-conscious about this, but most people don't notice it. It's something that can show up in photographs without being all that obvious in person. Perhaps it's become more noticeable in recent years.

It reminds me of the scar on my mother's neck, the scar that every violinist develops. A violinist tucks a handkerchief between her chin and chin rest, but a rough, reddened area gets scraped there anyway. It's a small sacrifice to the god of music, and string players don't give it a second thought.

We humans make all sorts of sacrifices to all sorts of gods. I half-think I had to see myself the way I did in order to avoid sorority rushes, even marriage to somebody famous. Now that I'm older and my face is a tad lopsided and I'm in no immediate danger from either sororities or famous men, I go outside whenever I want, sometimes without a stitch of makeup. Not long ago, I advised a younger woman to enjoy her good looks. "Don't feel guilty about being pretty," I said. "Don't beat yourself over the head for not deserving it. Enjoy it." All the same, I don't completely regret not having been able to enjoy my own. Those days I hid indoors, I got a lot of writing done; I wrote poems and stories and novels and more poems. I had my own god to sacrifice to.

That was always, I now remember, the beauty that most mattered to me, to my mother, too: the beauty of art (and is not any work done wholeheartedly, deliberately, and unself-consciously a work of art, and beautiful?). My mother may have wanted me to live a life she was too busy to live, but ironically we turned out to be too alike for that. Next to art's eternal truth, my mother already knew and I figured out, mortal beauty is as nothing. Nothing like art, which is beauty that creates itself by believing in something beyond itself.

MY MOTHER AND
MR. ALLEN DEWEY SPOONER

I can barely remember him, but I will never forget him. He was my mother's father. He died when I was seven. He died in Gulfport, Mississippi, at one end of the country, while I was a child in upstate New York at the far other end.

He was descended from Pilgrims. The first Spooner in America landed at Plymouth Rock in 1637. Allen Dewey Spooner was born in 1872 in Rensselaer Falls, New York, and grew up there, but his family moved south, and at twenty-three he was working for a lumber company in Lake Charles, Louisiana, where he met my grandmother Hattie, who called him "Allie." They were married—after some spectacular arguments between redheaded Hattie and Grandma LaBesse, who needed to be persuaded that a Yankee could be an acceptable suitor—and eventually my mother appeared on the scene, the youngest of three daughters, each of them so different from the other two that Hattie and Allen must have thought, sometimes, that random selection would have resulted in more uniformity. Perhaps the first one had scared Allen a little; fathers seem to be nervously cautious about the first daughter, unsure what to do with this appealing but undeniably alien creature. The second was a hell-raiser, destined from the day she was born to be a flapper in short skirts and long beads. My mother, of course, was his favorite. She was shy and smart and loved music and sent notes to him that read, "Would you like to have lunch with your daughter Mary?" He always wrote back, "It would be very fine indeed to have lunch with my daughter Mary." He was a saw filer, keeping the teeth of the giant saw impressively and precisely sharp, and they ate lunch on a tablecloth Mary spread over a broad, flat rock near the mill. He was the best filer in the business, it was said in that part of the country. This was a strange and beautiful part of the country, where huge cypresses immodestly revealed their roots, and hanging moss swayed back and forth like silent wind chimes, and a heavy aroma of sulphur lay on top of the still day, smothering it, clinging to people's throats like a scarf....

My mother had just been released from six weeks' quarantine in an upstairs bedroom that Hattie was now fumigating, to rid it of scarlet-fever germs. It was Sunday, and there were always callers on Sunday afternoon. Allen was in his Sunday suit, having played the organ prelude at First Presbyterian. After a midday dinner of crab gumbo and pot roast he would step into the parlor to select an afternoon's worth of symphonies from a stack of quarter-inch-thick Edison records that lay next to the only phonograph in Lake Charles. Despite Hattie's protestations, he remained convinced that intelligent visitors would rather listen to good music than make small talk, and he refused to give up this conviction even after he drove them out to the sun porch with his record of the entirely shocking new piece, *Le Sacre du Printemps*.

This day there was an uneasiness to the afternoon that even my five-year-old mother could sense. Everyone seemed on edge. There were rumors that a hurricane had devastated Grand Isle and might be headed for Lake Charles. For once, Allen did not object when Hattie asked him to turn off the phonograph. The sister who was going to be a flapper in just a few more years but was still in pinafore and pigtails peered out the parlor window. "Come look at the funny clouds," she begged everyone. Allen examined the barometer on the parlor wall. "She's falling, all right," he reported. "Better get ready for a little blow."

The conversation in the parlor turned to the war. It was 1917, and just the day before, a trainload of soldiers from nearby Gerstner Field had pulled out of town to the accompaniment of cheers and waving banners, and the town band, in which Allen played clarinet. Grandma LaBesse expressed displeasure with the neighborhood children for mocking poor old Professor Schultz and shouting "German spy! German spy!" as he shuffled along the sidewalk. Flags draped front porches; women rolled bandages for the Red Cross; and Mr. Cloony, the choir director, organized community "sings," flailing his arms enthusiastically while belting out the words to "It's a Long, Long Way to Tipperary" and "I'm Forever Blowing Bubbles." Everyone ridiculed the Kaiser and boasted of self-imposed privations. Mrs. Beardsley told the assemblage in the parlor how she had carried a case of railroad-salvage pork and beans all the way from the depot to the house in South Ryan Street, and Hattie explained, to their daughters' lasting horror, that the "scrambled eggs" they had eaten for supper the night before had really been *brains*.

After the guests left, the family went into the kitchen for a Sunday night supper of peanut butter and jelly sandwiches. Hattie didn't cook on Sunday nights. She would have liked to keep the entire Sabbath holy, but that was clearly impossible. Instead she managed, by getting up at 5 A.M., to free Sunday afternoons and evenings. From 5 A.M. until time to leave for church, she bustled about the kitchen, striving so zealously toward her half day of rest that God, one must believe, forgave her those few sinful hours of industry.

Just before dark the rain began to fall.

By morning, frenzied gusts of wind were slinging rain against the windows so hard that the panes shuddered and threatened to collapse. My mother crept downstairs to the kitchen, where oatmeal had been steaming all night in the "fireless cooker"—a double-welled cabinet with hot round slabs of stone at the bottoms of the wells. Allen motioned for her to sit down at the breakfast table while he read the scripture aloud, as he did every morning. Then Hattie read a prayer from a familiar booklet titled *Our Daily Bread*. It didn't matter that my mother didn't fully understand the scripture passages: Just the fact that her parents were seated there, so inseparable in their faith, lent stability to her small world.

But today, the ritual seemed somehow perfunctory, as if her parents were really thinking about something else. There was an impatience, an urgency in the room. As soon as she finished reading the prayer, Hattie told her daughters that they were not to go to school that day, and then Hattie resumed a discussion with Allen that had obviously been going on even before Mary had entered the room. She was pleading with him not to venture out in the boat—his only way of getting to the sawmill. "I *have* to go, Hattie," he said. "I have to warn Eddie and Jack to board up their houses and get to higher ground."

Eddie and Jack were Allen's helpers in the filing room. Jack, as Hattie pointed out, could take care of himself—or else his tattoos were a kind of false advertisement. But as much as she wanted her husband to stay home, she had to admit that the younger and more imaginative Eddie seemed a bit uncertain about how to deal with the real world. One Christmas, when Eddie went to the commissary to buy six monogrammed handkerchiefs for his boss, Mr. Allen Dewey Spooner, and discovered that the *S*'s were all sold out, he bought 3 *A*'s and 3 *D*'s.

After Allen left for the mill, Hattie paced the floor and watched the barometer. The wind had gotten worse. The top blew off the rabbit coop, and Mary, concerned for her pet rabbits, set up a howl that could be heard above the roar of the storm. Clinging to the fence and clothesline poles, her red hair flying in the wind like a cardinal on the wing, Hattie made her way to the coop, wrestled the top back on, and latched it securely. And then the wind got *worse*.

Windows were blown in as easily as if they'd been made of cellophane, the chimney crumpled as if it had been made of tissue paper, and the servants' house in the back yard toppled over. The mailman, conscientiously trying to make his rounds in the horse-drawn cart that had a little step on the back, where he stood, gave up just as he reached the Spooner residence. He brought his pouch into the parlor, spread the wet letters all over the imitation Persian rug, and carefully patted them dry. Every time a window blew in, Hattie and her daughters and the mailman would push a heavy piece of furniture up against the opening. Just when Hattie determined that they should all make a dash for the school building, a tin roof came hurtling past the house and she decided they'd better stay where they were.

Allen had designed and built his boat, *The Flick*, by himself. Her hull was the finest mahogany, her hardware solid brass, and the varnished canvas that covered her prow was smooth and tight. (*The Flick* frequently took top honors in exciting boat races at twenty-one miles an hour.) The route to the mill might have been considered by some to be hazardous even in good weather. Large and deep, Lake Charles was rough and gray and white-capped in stormy weather. From Lake Charles, Allen's route led him a short distance up Calcasieu River and then through a cut-off that provided a crossover to Prien Lake. The cut-off was like a miniature manmade bayou, the water blackened by the shadows of dense, overhanging vines and moss-covered trees whose branches dripped fat cream-colored snakes. Prien was dotted with islets, most of them nothing more than a few cypress trees surrounded by tall marsh grass and cattails. Herons stalked the shallows around the islet, searching, with dignified deliberation, for minnows, and kingfishers and sandpipers skittered along the edges. Prien appeared at first glance to be a navigator's nightmare, but its treacherous "stumps" invariably turned out to be alligator snouts that sank slowly and mysteriously out of sight when *The Flick* approached. From Prien, he had to go a short distance up yet another river to Lockport.

Despite the choppy water and rising wind, Allen made it safely to the mill. He moored in the boathouse and, drenched and bent double against the wind, walked up to the mill. An outside stairway led to the filing-room on the second floor. Eddie and Jack were there, but of course working had been out of the question; it was all they could do to move the machine tools away from the windows as the panes shattered on the filing-room floor. Sawdust, made amazingly painful by the force of wind, whirled through the air like a sandstorm and stung the men and lodged in their eyes and nostrils as they struggled with the heavy machinery.

Hurricanes usually dissipated fairly soon over land. Eddie and Jack had not really thought that this "squall" would turn out to be a full-fledged storm. Allen ordered them to leave at once. "You must tell the Cajun laborers to go home and protect their wives and children," he explained. The men left, grateful. In those days, storm warnings could reach the bayous only by word of mouth; there were no radios or newspapers in remote areas.

Behind the sawmill was a slag heap—a great pile of burning wood scraps and sawdust that rose almost to the level of the mill's roof. It smoldered night and day, giving off an eerie glow and occasionally sending up showers of sparks and hissing snake-tongues of flames when the wind touched it. Even the rain from the storm could not put out the fire that was deep within it, as alive and red as a heart. Suddenly a tremendous gust, a mighty rogue rush, ripped the smoldering heap apart and carried blazing debris to the mill, igniting the roof. The fire, whipped about by the wind, shot up to the sky. The rickety wooden building, its timbers parched by summer temperatures, flared up almost in one spontaneous burst of flame. Then the sparks leaped to the adjacent lumberyard, where stacks of rich pine boards glistened with amber beads of resin drawn out of the wood by the intense heat. Raindrops sputtered and fizzled, powerless against the fire. Allen—he could not say how he found the strength—picked up his heavy chest of treasured hand tools and flung it through a window. Then he ran down the wooden steps, reaching the ground just as the flames roared up behind him to engulf the stairway and, dragging his tool box, made his way slowly to the boathouse. As he looked back over his shoulder at the mill burning to the ground, he thanked God that he had sent Eddie and Jack away.

Once in the boat, his tool chest stowed securely in the back seat, Allen didn't know whether to start for home or sit it out. The storm had apparently reached its height and the wind seemed now to be dying down. He recognized this as the eye of the hurricane and made up his mind to head for home in the hope of getting there before the eye could pass over and the storm regain its impetus. But in his eagerness he backed out of his shelter a few minutes too soon, and as he sped down river to Prien Lake, a flying piece of timber struck *The Flick* and punched a gaping hole in her side above the water line. Only his intimate knowledge of the waters through which he passed enabled him to make the trip home. As he reached the front door, which had been knocked askew and given a permanently crazy look by winds that hit 150 miles per hour, Hattie flung it open and cried "Oh, Allie!" throwing herself joyfully into his arms.

Allen and Hattie worked hard all their lives and never missed a single Sunday at church, but they also loved dancing to Strauss waltzes. Allen enjoyed photography and fishing, and after he bought his first automobile, a Model-T Ford, he took his family on trips to see the sulphur mountains and the red-pepper fields and the tropical-bird sanctuary and the sugar-cane fields. They visited a salt mine, and a plantation that had survived The War Between the States, as he and Hattie called it.

When he was seventy-four and Hattie was sixty-eight, he drove her from Gulfport to upstate New York. He was already dying of cancer, but this was their "honeymoon"—better late than never. They even went to Niagara Falls. That summer, our family was staying in a dilapidated house on Lake Rousseau in Canada, where chipmunks actually scampered around the kitchen. Allen and Hattie drove to Canada, bringing gifts for the grandchildren. While my mother, now a beautiful young

woman and professional violinist, was chatting away with her
mother, the elderly gentleman we'd been told to call "Grandpa"
set the toys down on the floor in front of us and watched us from
a straight-back chair. In front of me was a sizable glass fire truck
filled with tiny, brilliantly colored candies. I was four and had
never seen such an entrancing thing as this fire truck.

What I remember about him, that elderly gentleman sitting
so straightly on the ladderback chair, is how his shadow seemed
to fold itself around me, like the wings of a watchful angel. What
I remember is how my mother, whose life, finally, did not turn
out as happily as she might have wished, could always be made
happier by the thought of her parents, but especially the thought
of her father. Her face, when she had become old in her own turn
and reminisced about her parents, but especially about her father,
seemed to light up, like a candle one lights in loving memory.

THE MEANING OF GUILT

Does guilt serve a purpose? Or is it merely a rationale for living our lives the way we would anyway, a complicated psychological ornament (say, a hair shirt) for the body's own will? Can there be redemption without the idea of guilt? What, precisely, is atonement? Anne Tyler's twelfth novel takes on these questions but prefers not to pursue them through metaphorical or philosophical analysis. Rather, the questions are functions of the narrative. Though the text never, really, explores them, the narrative continually, almost relentlessly, thrusts them at the reader. The reader, meanwhile, is enthralled, for the narrative is utterly involving and affecting, creating for itself the degree of plausibility that first-rate books stubbornly continue to achieve even in an era of deconstructionism and minimalism, but those questions— Those questions remain. They are not answered. Or if what I read as ambiguity is not that but an answer indeed, then they are answered with a flippancy so disturbing and implicative that, at book's end, the reader comes face to face with a darkness far greater than the darkness that propels the narrative into existence.

A young man, a teenager in fact, at a time when he is discovering sex with his girlfriend and becoming wise, he believes, in the ways of the world, informs his older brother that the brother's new baby daughter, born, to the bemusement of the Bedloe family—Anne Tyler's latest family of subjects—on the younger brother's birthday and presumably two months premature but clearly fully developed, is not his older brother's.

"She was somebody else's," Ian said.

"Come again?"

"I just want to know how long you intend to be a fall guy," Ian said.

Danny turned onto Waverly and drew up in front of the house. He cut the engine and looked over at Ian. He seemed entirely sober now. He said, "What are you trying to tell me, Ian?"

"She's out all afternoon any time she can get a sitter," Ian said. "She comes back perfumed and laughing and wearing clothes she can't afford. That white knit dress. Haven't you ever seen her white dress? Where'd she get it? How'd she pay for it? How come she married you quick as a flash and then had a baby just seven months later?"

Danny is supposed to wait while Ian runs into the Bedloe house to root through his closet for the packet of rubbers he has hidden in a gym shoe; this is to be "[t]he biggest night of [Ian's] life." He stops in the bathroom to comb his hair. As he is considering himself in the mirror, he hears a car crash. Danny is dead.

Thus the book begins, predicated quite literally on accident, as if the first chaos, scrambling itself without rhyme or reason into ever greater complication, were necessarily to result in patterning, the possibilities for meaninglessness being far more limited than the possibilities for meaning. Perhaps this is why the reader of this book looks for meaning—not, of course, *a* meaning, for propaganda is not what's wanted, but an affirmation of the reality of meaning. There is a sense, here at the book's beginning, where misery is heaped on misery in Job-like fashion, that all of this must lead somewhere meaningful. For soon Danny's wife, who, it's revealed later, had not been having an affair during her marriage but making shoplifting excursions with a girlfriend, overdoses on sleeping pills, leaving two small children from an earlier marriage, Agatha and Thomas, and Daphne, the child Danny had thought was his, to be raised, it turns out, by the Bedloes, and in particular by Ian, who drops out of college after his first semester to undertake this task in a spirit of penance.

The Bedloes are the kind of family who are aware of themselves as a family unit. "They believed that every part of their lives was absolutely wonderful. . . . Or at least Ian's mother did, and she was the one who set the tone." But finally even Bee cannot deny the truth to herself, and a day comes when, in a speech addressed to her husband, Doug, that seems also directed at the reader, she speaks it:

> "Sometimes I have the strangest feeling. I give this start and I think 'Why!' I think, 'Why, here we are! Just going about our business the same as usual!' And yet so much has changed. Danny is gone, our golden boy, our first baby boy that we were so proud of, and our house is stuffed with someone else's children. You know they *all* are someone else's. You know that! And Ian is a whole different person and Claudia's so bustling now and our lives have turned so makeshift and second-class, so second-string, so second-fiddle, and everything's been lost. Isn't it amazing that we keep on going? That we keep on shopping for clothes and getting hungry and laughing at jokes on TV? When our oldest son is dead and gone and we'll never see him again and our life's in ruins!"
>
> "Now, sweetie," he said.
>
> "We've had such extraordinary troubles," she said,

"and somehow they've turned us ordinary. That's what's
so hard to figure. We're not a special family anymore."

That they are not special (but of course, we are meant to realize
that all families, happy and unhappy alike, are special) works
to this novel's advantage: what we have here is more than
a collection of quirky characters.   It is a gathering up of souls
in distress.   Tyler's rendering of each of them is superb: Ian,
who may or may not be engaged in a pilgrim's progress; Bee
and Doug, the bewildered parents; Agatha and Thomas, the
Gretel and Hansel who, acutely aware of the precariousness of
their situation in life, perceive in Ian a path to safety; Danny;
Danny's wife, Lucy, whose sexual vibrancy Ian, in the heightened
hormonal condition of adolescence, cannot help but respond to,
surely coveting his brother's wife.   "*That V neckline,*" he thinks
helplessly, as she models the white knit dress for him, "*plunging
so low in the middle.   And that skirt that whisks around your legs
and makes that shimmery sound.*"   Ian's sexual attraction to Lucy,
which he never quite dares to deal with consciously, supplies the
grounding—the *Bedloe*, I want to say—that allows us to accept
as believable his renunciation, for much of his life, of sex.   Tyler
does not flag this connection—of sexuality to celibacy—for the
reader, but it's there, and useful.   Without it, we might not doubt
Ian's conversion, but we would be perplexed by the particularities
of his spiritual allegiance, which, as it is, we are glad to consent to
(but not take on faith).

If there is a member of the family who remains opaque, it
is not Claudia, the mostly offstage sister, but Daphne, whose
casual bed- and job-hopping and colorful clothing too generically
refer to an entire generation.   Rita, who enters the book late, is
also stereotypical, an earth mother who, the family members
generally agree, with relief, has rescued Ian from himself.   But all
of the characters hold the reader in an embrace so warm that it
seems to be a promise of something.   *Something meaningful.*

And so the reader keeps looking for it.   Is it to be found
where Ian seeks it, in the Church of the Second Chance?   Having
experienced a spiritual rebirth during the funeral service for Lucy,

when "it seemed the congregation was a single person—someone
of great kindness and compassion, someone gentle and wise and
forgiving," Ian wishes to replicate the experience; his search brings
him to Reverend Emmett's "religion of atonement and complete
forgiveness" and to the belief that he must change his life, at the
age of nineteen, to accommodate three homeless children. Is
meaning to be sought in allegory, or allegorical allusion, as when
Ian becomes a professional carpenter? But almost as soon as
anything so metaphysically expressive as a symbol appears the
plot turns a cold shoulder to it, whether out of disdain or lack
of interest or even a kind of nervousness. At the same time, it is
amazing that the twenty-five years that the book covers leave no
historical imprint on the page. Except for a few vague nods in its
direction—such as a comment on the "leggy look of the sixties"
as manifest in an old photograph of Lucy—history seems to be
something that has been happening elsewhere, not on Waverly
Street. Essentially, there are no presidents, no wars, no women's
movement, no civil rights movement, no Mideast crisis, no
anything beyond the domestic purview, in this novel. And this
is not a criticism, but it is a curious fact, and it suggests that, to
some degree, this book is defined by its absences.

Absent is the outside world. (Yes, foreigners appear, with
accents, but they carry no weight of reference.) Absent is any
interest at all in language or metaphor. (Sentences are interrupted
by a hiccupy use of parentheses within which information that
ought to have been folded into the narrative or dialogue is
burped up.) Anne Tyler is a master of narration and, usually,
characterization, and these make the novel a compelling one.
Absent is an authorial vision. Or is it?

Ian, who, like most teenagers, imagines that he is destined for
great things ("He was a medium kind of guy, all in all. Even so,
there were moments when he believed that someday, somehow,
he was going to end up famous"), is hounded by guilt into a life
of obscurity and self-abnegation, though it is also possible that
Tyler is having a little joke at the reader's expense here, since the
novelist is the biographer of fictional characters, and a 250,000-
copy first printing (so I read somewhere) pretty well guarantees

that Ian will be famous. But no, I don't think this is a joke; I think Ian is meant to be an average teenager who, despite Bee's outburst, becomes extraordinary in his resolute refusal to demand anything for himself.

A friend of mine likes to suggest an advertisement for guilt: "Guilt—the gift that keeps on giving." Guilt has gotten a bad name in our culture but perhaps this is another joke that is not altogether a joke. In this book, guilt often seems a lot like love. To be aware of one's own sinfulness—one's original sin—and to make one's whole life an act of contrition is not the worst that a person can do. It may be the best that anybody can do.

Ian is called "Saint Maybe" by Daphne because, in her eyes, he is cautious, always thinking in terms of the need for safety— or salvation. "I'm not like you," Daphne declares, in a sixteen-year-old's hurry to establish her individuality within the family. "King Careful. Mr. Look-Both-Ways. Saint Maybe." But he has not always been cautious; he threw aside conventional pleasures to abide by the rules of a religious community, the church. When he finds for himself, at last, the satisfactions of marriage and fatherhood, the reader feels, at first, happy for him. *Maybe there isn't a heaven*—a reader may be forgiven for thinking—*but at least he's gotten to participate in some of the joys of life on earth.* And then that bizarre thing happens, that stroke from nowhere: Ian, remembering how Danny had introduced his fiancée to his family by saying "I'd like you to meet the woman who's changed my life," imagines the young Lucy from so long ago thinking that "this was an ordinary occurrence. People changed other people's lives every day of the year. There was no call to make such a fuss about it." And all at once the book disappears, blown into nothingness by the most whimsical of breezes.

Or does it? Is this an ambiguity that is being sustained, a contradiction that is being supported by the artistic creation of the book? Shall we go away from a reading of the book thinking that life is both important *and* trivial, comic *and* tragic, that it is redeemed by good works *and* grace? Maybe.

Or was all that pain, that guilt, to no purpose at all, as unnecessary as self-flagellation? Maybe. Maybe everything that was predicated on accident has itself been accidental. Maybe guilt is, then, a luxury item, like a hair shirt purchased at some Saks Fifth Avenue of the soul. A mental flourish, an un-grace note.

Or was all that pain and guilt, in the end, so acridly dark as to be as difficult to comprehend as Job's misfortunes, the idea of a universe that *chooses* to visit its creatures with evil being even more unfathomable than a universe that has no consciousness of good and evil? Do we live in a universe where faith is possible only if morality is not? Maybe.

Saint Maybe.

Or do we have here simply an abdication of the author's responsibility to achieve a coherent vision, if not of the world, at least of the world of her book? Or does the author's vision in fact lie in her profound disinclination to suggest a reading of the world? I don't know.

I don't know the answers to any of these questions. What I do know, certainly, is that reading *Saint Maybe* is a wonderful way to live for a day or two or three. I know that Agatha and Thomas, Doug and Danny, especially, are presented with such feeling that a reader would have to be bored with living not to respond to them. I know that Ian is a character that the reader comes to love in the way that the children come to love him, with a love that is protective and appreciative but also "pale and flawed," because it is human love, not divine love. Daphne, realizing this about herself, finds that it makes "her want to weep for him." Here, for me, in retrospect, is the most marvelous moment in this book. It is as if Anne Tyler has held a mirror to our mortal fallibility, our inability to love one another perfectly. We gaze into this mirror, like Ian gazing into the bathroom mirror on "[t]he biggest night of his life," and what we see of ourselves is so pathetic and incomplete that our strongest desire is to save the world from ourselves.

SELF AND STRANGENESS

My high school history teachers never managed to get up to World War II before the school year came to a close. No matter how far we'd gotten—say it was April, and we were studying the League of Nations, or May and reading about the Oklahoma Dust Bowl—the events of the past stretched themselves out just long enough to let school end before the war, in the remaining chapter, began.

Later on, after I'd learned a little more history, I used to think that this was because my high school was in the South and my teachers didn't know how, or were afraid, to talk about race and culture.

Now, still later on, and seeing how my own students think that the Vietnam War is history whereas to me it is a still-present part of my life, I think maybe World War II just was not yet historical to my teachers.

I attended a county high school in Virginia when Virginia was ranked second from the bottom in public education. My biology teacher, a bachelor who tooled around in a red convertible, was fired for teaching the theory of evolution. My parents said the people who fired him were the proof that humans had not evolved. I needed permission from home to check *An American Tragedy* out of the school library. Of course, my parents gave me carte blanche. I read all the time.

We didn't have a television. Money was a concern. Working their regular jobs, giving quartet concerts, my parents took the exams and started an insurance agency on the side. Most of their clients were black people who were turned down by other agencies.

My parents finally purchased a television when I was in college. I was seventeen. I had finished my first year and was killing the summer at home before transferring to the New Mexico Institute of Mining and Technology, which was mostly my mother's idea. I used to stay up late reading the catalogues of colleges to which I was not allowed to apply: Vassar and Swarthmore were my favorites, but my parents thought it would be foolish to spend that much money on a school where all you would be doing was reading. You could read for free in a library.

One night, after we had the television set and before I left for New Mexico, and having sadly put the college catalogues away, I stayed up to watch an old movie that starred Gregory Peck.

The movie, based on a book, was *Gentlemen's Agreement*. In it, a Gentile reporter pretends to be a Jew in order to discover and expose anti-Semitism in the community. I found the movie disturbing, and instead of going to bed I slept downstairs in the dining room, curled up in the armchair, the better to catch my father before he left for work in the morning. I woke up when I heard him come down the stairs. "Dad," I asked, even before he could get to the kitchen, "why would Jews not be allowed to join a club?"

Perhaps a writer thinking about race in the South is expected to address relations between black and white people, but I want to start here, with Jews.

I had known some black people. My best friend when we lived for five years up North was a black girl named Mary Elizabeth.

In her bedroom, Mary Elizabeth had one of the most wonderful objects I had so far seen in my life: a bank in the shape of an owl. The owl had big wise eyes, and when you dropped a penny in the back of its head, the eyes closed, then opened even wider and briefly lit up. We'd spend an entire afternoon putting a penny in, making the owl blink, shaking the bank to make the penny fall out onto the bed and then putting the same penny back in.

And when my family moved back south, spending the first year in a tenant house on a farm, the black girls from the other tenant house chased my sister and me off the dirt road and called us names because—well, my sister and I didn't know why. They just didn't like or approve of us.

But I had never known a Jew, or if I had I'd not realized it and, as I say, I also had never gotten to the end of the history book. I trailed my father into the kitchen, where he made himself a cup of coffee. Before instant coffee became widely available, he used to mail-order coffee from Louisiana so he could get it with chicory. "Daddy," I asked, while he was still blowing on his coffee to get it cool enough to drink, "what, exactly, is a concentration camp?"

What he told me seemed almost too strange to be believed. Who would want to kill Jews for being Jews? In our family, Jew was synonymous with *smart*. Jew was synonymous with *good musician*.

Within two months of this conversation, I was engaged to a Jewish graduate student at New Mexico Tech. He was doing research in atmospheric physics. Instead of an engagement ring he gave me a piece of lightning trapped in a plastic cube.

Don't ask me what this meant or even how he got the lightning inside the cube—I was still just a sophomore ("sophomoron," a friend says), studiously drawing vectors in my physics-lab notebook, and I knew only that I possessed a thunderbolt. A thunderbolt! It had to be superior to a ring. Any girl could wear a ring.

This engagement lasted, I think, one week, but it made an impression on me so that when I was, myself, in graduate school, in North Carolina, and a young Jewish artist named Jonathan

Silver appeared on the scene, I got engaged again, and this time there was a wedding.

And a ring.

The wedding was sparsely attended, because Jonathan's family disowned him for marrying me. Naturally, my father then threatened to punch out his father. Jonathan's brother conferred with my brother. His mother sent best wishes but stayed away, just as her husband had ordered her to. My mother wondered how any woman could be such a wimp. In the midst of all this, Jonathan and I were pronounced man and wife, borrowed my father's car to drive off in, and checked into the Honeymoon Suite at the Thomas Jefferson Hotel in downtown Richmond. That night, we were hit by a blizzard, and the next day, on the way back, we drove into a ditch.

Which is pretty much what you could say about the whole marriage.

A couple of weeks before the wedding, while Jonathan and I were sitting at the kitchen table at my parents' house in Richmond, my mother had said she thought he and I should be apprised of a situation we might face. She disappeared into the dining room, rummaged through a drop-leaf desk, and returned with the deed to the house. This particular house was the fourth and last one my parents had in Richmond, the one they'd saved all their money for. "Read this," my mother said, pointing to the small print.

Property in that subdivision, which had been annexed to the city of Richmond, was under no circumstances to be sold or leased to non-Aryan persons.

"On one hand," my mother said, "it doesn't mean anything and everyone knows it doesn't mean anything. It's a pro forma clause, irrelevant to any real situation. On the other hand, it means, and everyone knows it means, that black people are not allowed to live here. Who knows what it could mean, if someone tested it? And on the third hand, it means, even if nobody has ever thought about this, that the two of you would not be allowed to buy a house here either."

My mother did not say this to scare us. She was an energetic soul who liked nothing better than a good fight. She was not interested in keeping up with the Joneses, because she had only contempt for the Joneses. Nobody ever told *her* what to do. For example, it was about this time that my parents were invited to attend a choral concert at an all-black church in downtown Richmond. In the sixties, the invitation was a considerable honor. Members of the church wanted to say thanks for the courageous way my parents had represented them in insurance transactions.

My mother finished her speech. Then, having exactly zero money and no expectation of owning a home anywhere, Jonathan and I laughed simultaneously.

"I just wanted you to know what you're getting into," my mother said.

Perhaps we still didn't know *that*, but though Jonathan and I laughed my mother had succeeded in making us realize, with a sudden sharpness, what it means to be a second-class citizen. The feeling reminded me of College Day For High School Students, which was held at the good school inside the city limits. I'd managed to get a ride, skipping classes at my county school. I was fifteen, and another of the colleges I dreamed of was Princeton—because that's where the Institute for Advanced Study was, and the Institute was where Einstein was. I went up to the Princeton booth. Teenaged boys and blazered college reps looked at me as if I were crazy. I stated my mission. The boys and the reps hooted. If it had not been so un-Princetonian, they would have slapped their khaki-clad thighs. "A girl!" they said. "A girl wants to go to Princeton!"

These things—race, gender, class—become so mixed up that it is impossible to separate them out. Did Jonathan seem to me an ally against a world of WASP privilege? Was I drawn to him out of, in part, a sense of guilt for the transgressions of history? Did we founder because I was angry with a category of human beings—men—for having control over my life? Or because I was, amazingly, too *obedient* to him, this one individual man, relinquishing control (for that was also true, to my mother's distress)?

A writer raises these questions in disguised ways, weaving them into the very fabric of her fabrications. All my novels are somewhat about money, or the lack thereof. One unpublished and one published novel wrestle with issues of racial integration, and another published novel, *Augusta Played*, treats of, among other things, Judaism. In every fictional work, there is for the writer the problem of point of view. Whose point of view will she use, and why?

At the outset of *The Second Sex*, which remains and will remain an extraordinary book no matter how many revisionist biographies of its author may be published, Simone de Beauvoir states, "Otherness is a fundamental category of human thought," remarking that the duality of Self and Other was not, in the beginning, sexed.

For a writer, Self and Other *are* sexed. (And one means, here, sexed and not merely *gendered*.) A writer, obliged to select a point of view, has to choose between a male and a female point of view or else write something extremely experimental. (*Middlesex*, by Jeffrey Eugenides, is narrated by a hermaphrodite. Still, she/ he is by turns herself and himself.) When I look back at the poems and fictions I wrote before I began to publish much, I find that most of them adopted a male point of view. A sinister male protagonist named Dev chills a young female character's heart with his erotic nihilism. A sinister red-headed male protagonist goes to Mexico for the Days of the Dead and experiences a Thomas Mann-like baring of his essential self. A younger, but still sinister, male protagonist who lives out in the country paints his more-or-less-oblivious (she's very sound asleep) pregnant wife a bright orange. An even younger male protagonist, named Rubicon Bright because he is smart and has a Rubicon to cross, is not himself sinister but everyone around him is. And *he* probably *will* be, when he enters Rome.

Recently I stumbled across this shrewd observation by Joanna Russ, who is speaking about the female writer writing from a male point of view:

She is an artist creating a world in which persons of her kind cannot be artists, a consciousness central to itself creating a world in which women have no consciousness, a successful person creating a world in which persons like herself cannot be successes. She is a self trying to pretend that she is a different Self, one for whom her own self is Other.

I wish someone had explained Russ's point to me in time to spare me years of wasted effort, years when I was writing falsehood rather than fiction. And yet, and yet. What young writer can fail to be thrilled by the magnificent aim of renouncing the Self for the sake of the expression of the Other? Keats, we all know, located greatness in "Negative Capability, . . .when man is capable of being in uncertainties, Mysteries, doubts, without any irritable reaching after fact & reason." For Keats, a great writer was one who was willing to forego a point of view in order to render other points of view fully.

Here, then, are two poles of thought, and these days it may sometimes seem that a writer, especially a female writer, is being asked to hang herself between them. A female writer wants to imagine the world as it may exist for an Other—a male self, or a black or Jewish self, perhaps a self whose economic background is unlike her own. She wants to do this because she wants to know a wide world and she wants to know it intimately, and because she comes to understand her own point of view better by understanding other points of view, but also because fiction is, first of all, fiction. Fiction *is* falsehood, and what was wrong with my sinister male protagonists was simply that they were incompletely imagined. I didn't know a lot about men, and I knew even less about sinisterness. It will seem ironic, to a female writer wanting to seize the same rights to ambition as have been traditionally granted to the male writer, that contemporary critics of literature condemn her for "appropriating" experience that "belongs" to someone else. A writer is told she must not explore the experience of people whose skin color differs from hers. An American writer is told she must not explore third-world experience. Sylvia Plath is anathematized for attempting what, in a kinder light, may be seen as a very young writer's empathic, if arguably clumsy, memorialization of Holocaust experience. Experience becomes a boutique commodity, something like a pair of designer shoes, and nobody gets to walk in anybody else's shoes.

And yet and yet. The woman writer wants to be faithful to her own consciousness, for her experience is different from anyone else's and especially from men's experience. She agrees that she has a special responsibility to convey her experience precisely because it has for so long been marginalized and may therefore, unless she takes steps to see that it is not, be overlooked. History imposes obligations, of which this seems to her to be one. Moreover, experience, her experience, has taught her that if she is not careful she may dissolve her Self in the acids of desire, wanting always to be who or what she is not. There is a longing to escape the Self that is so great that it may appear to be a kind of philosophy when, really, it is only boredom, frustration, or self-contempt. A writer must find a way to be both true to herself and free of herself.

Here is everything I know, whether it is sufficient or not, about how this is to be done: To begin with, the writer needs to acquire mastery of techniques, and in my opinion, the more techniques the better. The goal is a confidence that permits forgetfulness: The writer can now focus her attention on her subject. And in the second place, a writer needs to deepen her acquaintance with this self of hers with which she is seeking to establish a working relationship. If she does, she will find that, no matter how different the Other, at first glance, seems, it is inevitably the Self that is lastingly exotic, sometimes alienating, and, for sure, as strange as an unidentified species. It is the Self, protean and, so to speak, submarine, that tempts us to dangerous, unfathomable depths. Here we encounter a solitude as huge as if it contained creation and as local, concentrated, and unrelieved as if all the layers of creation weighed on it. Nearly, but not quite, overwhelmed, we reach out to an Other to share an identity.

There are many wonderful contemporary black women writers, not all of whom are as well known as they deserve to be (read Becky Birtha, Nettie Jones, ZZ Packer!). Here are just four of them:

Colleen J. McElroy, known first as a fine poet, is also the author of *Jesus and Fat Tuesday and Other Short Stories*. Astonishingly ambitious, this collection spans American history from 1882 (in the first story, Cressy, born "two years after the Civil War," is fifteen) to the present. Black people in these stories move from near-slavery to the middle class to Muslim revolution to near-equality (though the women remain subject to sexual thralldom, about which McElroy writes as convincingly as anyone). In other words, what we have here is a history of black life in America—a hundred years of black social history–in two hundred pages. But nothing is skimped, neither narrative nor language.

This is anti-minimalist fiction, fiction that pushes itself beyond the fashionably truncated climax, even beyond the conventional close, to another, unanticipated point. While I can't quote an entire story, a passage from near the end of "The Limitations of Jeremy Packard" offers an idea of McElroy's narrative sweep:

> For a while, he managed to snag odd jobs in some of the joints he and Buford had worked, but always, the piano betrayed him and he'd end the night picking away at notes that had no melody except madness. On those nights, Jason dreamed of Regina. . . .
>
> Somewhere in the quagmire of Market Street stores, fresh air fruit stands, loading docks, and bars, Jason Packard grew old. . . .

McElroy uses her poetic ear to her stories' advantage. A rich, even extravagant rhetoric deepens and expands her meaning. At the same time, as becomes a poet, she anchors her rhetoric with the unarguable reality of sensory detail. Regina's black crystal beads "seemed to gather all the light bleeding through the milky leaded glass of the front door panel." In "More Than a Notion," Josephine, a narrator who, like several characters, recurs in various stories, observes that

> [w]hen Papa was around, the house smelled of peppermint and heavy smoke from his last cigar mingled with an odor that Mama, Margay or Aunt Fern can't even come close to. They're filled with the traces of what women are. Food, babies and perfume. Bits and pieces of sewing thread and furniture polish, hair oil, spicy soap, last night's supper, or maybe even some man they've rubbed against. Women have smells that float around them like clouds, but a man is a mass of separate smells that push against each other like muscles....

In "A House Full of Maude," there is "[a] kitchen where bacon was fried, even at night, its smokehouse odors barely masking cigarettes and whiskey, chitterlings and jars of pickling. And none of it as pungent as the pomade on the back burner where Maude hot-cooked her hair before choir practice." (I've seldom read a writer so good at conjuring smells. James Joyce was good at it.)

This language, these details are in the service here of many points of view—male and female, young and old, historical and contemporary. McElroy is a writer of exceptional reach, with the technical versatility to realize her intentions. She can make a character say "Let's show Nab some tail feathers and floorboard these hogs." She can say of another character in another story that she "had screamed so long, her voice broke and vanished in her throat like water sucked into a downspout." *Jesus and Fat Tuesday* belongs to the invaluable class of books that surprise us with the testimony of our own senses, our own intelligence, making us aware of what we know, or can know if we pay attention.

Gayl Jones's novel *Corregidora* (it was her first) is a book about the blues: singing them, living them. When the words are right, the downbeat lifts you up and pulls you in.

In 1947 Ursa Corregidora, the narrator-protagonist, is singing at Happy's Café. The year is important because it's pre-Pill. A central theme here is the advice handed down by the women in Ursa's family, "to make generations." That's a theme for a blues song if ever there was one, especially since Ursa's jealous first husband, Mutt Thomas, grabbing her backstage to complain that the men at Happy's "mess with they eyes," causes her to fall, lose the baby she's carrying, and undergo a hysterectomy. She's twenty-five, and so angry that she curses everyone in sight.

The women in Ursa's family perversely insist on keeping the name of their Portuguese master-lover-father: Corregidora. The patriarch, vicious and well-nigh inescapable, raised his daughters to work as whores—and to minister to his own needs, too. Perhaps pain itself recedes into the past; the Corregidora women are unwilling to forgive, or forget, the sheer *indignity* of their suffering. "I'm leaving evidence," Great Gram tells little Ursa. "And you got to leave evidence too. And your children got to leave evidence. And when it come time to hold up the evidence, we got to have evidence to hold up." But Ursa is not going to have any children, and in a way, this is her real liberation, the release from specific, traditional hatred into a magnanimous sense of irony which, like death, is a great equalizer. Reunited with Mutt at book's close, Ursa goes down on him, always the friendliest sexual gesture since it holds such possibility for revenge. "I don't want a kind of woman that hurt you," Mutt says, and Ursa, crying, finally admits with matching humility, "I don't want a kind of man that'll hurt me neither."

On the relations between men and women—Ursa and Mutt, Ursa and Tadpole McCormick, Ursa's mother and father, lesbian Cat Lawson and her husband, Joe Hunn, who once replaced the broken window of his car with a Kotex box—Gayl Jones is perceptive and understanding. She writes well about sex and even better about the way men and women misuse each other out of bed.

But seeking significance, she can go off the deep end. There are italicized passages where the language collapses into unintended comedy. "My breasts quiver like old apples." And, "I'll make a fetus out of grounds of coffee to rub inside my eyes." Or again, "We're all consequences of something. . . .It ain't a pussy down there, it's a whole world," Ursa thinks, feeling "bruised" by sperm. The Greeks may have been right after all, attributing female hysteria to a wandering womb.

The best parts of Jones's book are like Ursa's singing after her operation. "It sounded like it had sweat in it." For it is the life behind the life that you make art from, "the lived life, not the spoken one." Not the life recounted in a litany of grievances, not talk of "making generations," but the life lived by a beat-up, beat-down, singular woman, such as Ursa's mother walking home holding her purple slacks up after her husband has yanked the elastic waistband out. Or Ursa herself, finding her second husband, Taddy, with a "pretty little thing," Vivian. Or Ursa singing.

Time passes, and how it passes—deceptively—is one of the interesting things in this book. In 1969 Ursa is working at another place, the Spider. She's forty-seven, an unusual age for an American woman to be in fiction. The question life hasn't yet answered for her is the one about Corregidora: "What is it a woman can do to a man that make him hate her so bad he wont [sic] to kill her one minute and keep thinking about her and can't get her out of his mind the next?" In the final scene, Jones grants Ursa's husband a moment of grace as Mutt, confessing to mortality and sin but on those very counts acquitted of Corregidora's crimes, embraces his wife. Jones's evidence is her book: it accuses, it weeps.

Beginning her career in dazzling brightness, her college education sponsored by Elizabeth Hardwick, who arranged a scholarship for this talented student, Gayl Jones moved in the direction of radicalism. In the nineties her husband killed himself during a shootout with police. Her personal pain can only be imagined, but whatever other journeys Jones has made, she has continued her journey as a writer and by now has achieved an oeuvre. She is making music out of history.

Accustomed as all of us in this country are—and as no doubt it is instructive for us to be—to the rhetoric of rage, some may find *Through the Ivory Gate*, the first novel by the second African-American to win a Pulitzer prize for poetry, almost shocking in its sweet optimism, its willingness to forgive. Here is narrative prose whose first impulse is to describe its world precisely, without preconception. Such writing is felt by the reader as a kind of caress. It is as if the book reaches out to all its readers, saying *Join me in this venture; we're side by side here.*

I do not suggest that Rita Dove fails to address important issues of race, for race is central to her heroine's predicament. Virginia King, a puppeteer in residence in Akron, Ohio, as an Artist-in-the-Schools, had been drawn first to music and studied the cello; in college in Wisconsin, she became a drama major (courageously insisting on her right to study mime), but when she had difficulty finding roles for black women, she joined an experimental puppet troupe. After a prologue, it is in Akron with her puppets that we find her.

In the prologue, we have met Virginia in childhood—in the same city of Akron, before her family moved to Arizona—and watched as she hurled out the window the "Negro baby doll" her grandmother had given her. Through subsequent years in Arizona, and college and a commune in the midwest, Virginia's progress is away from self-hatred toward a state of independence, a place in the world and her mind where she can delight in being herself.

And what an intriguing young woman she is, this student of Bach and Brecht who also cares about her family and friends and the children she brings the magic of theater to, who, even though she remembers when a childhood friend called her "Nigger," grows close to her white roommate in college but reserves Saturday afternoons for visiting with her black girlfriends, "scattered like raisins among the white swirls of coeds during the week," and who falls in love, the first time, like just about every woman of just about any race, with a man who cannot help but break her heart.

At every point, Dove helps us to see Virginia's life as clearly as if we were living it. We see "the nine o'clock sun pressed flat into the pasty sky." A neighbor has upper arms "spongy as Wonder bread." We hear music like "a leaf shaken of the last rain." There is "a chilling drizzle that drifted under the umbrella, coating her sweater with a glaze of pearly mist, like a long cool drink for one's pores." Virginia's passion may be for "dreams of glimmering illusion" that enter or emerge through the ivory gate, but Dove's descriptive writing makes us believe in their reality, the thing-ness of them. At moments her writing about music becomes music, "the true music that gripped and made pride bow down before the monumental sadness of being alive, music that required no explication, no translation."

As is true of all progress, Virginia's progress is also from a history of hurt to a new hopefulness. In returning to her hometown, she undertakes a journey of discovery. A family secret is revealed—the family secret, the hidden truth that had divided her parents, Ernest and Belle, plunging them into isolating despair.

It was some strange grief, maybe the same grief that paralyzed her father at the kitchen table, his brow bent over his clenched hands long after grace was said, the same grief that turned Belle's gaze inward and made her talk to the unborn child when she thought no one was listening. Maybe it was even the sadness Virginia and Ernie Jr. felt at leaving Akron for a place that looked like the moon.

But her grandmother explains, "You see, if you're one of the damaged, you have to confront the damage to find out what you can use before you put the rest away. There's always something you can use." In art and life, it is clear, Virginia will find a use for what she learns.

Throughout the novel Dove alternates past and present, Virginia's return to Akron layered like a cake with returns via recollection to childhood and college. No irony distracts us from our engagement with these events, narrated or remembered. In fact, it is a pleasure to read a contemporary novel that does not depend on irony to establish a sense of collusion or complicity between author and reader. And it may be this lack of irony that accounts for the certain sweet purity (not puritanism) that suffuses the story, runs through like a melodic line—and it is a relief, too, from postmodernism's insistence on being in the know, one up, too cool *for words*.

Dove's Pulitzer prize-winning poetry collection *Thomas and Beulah*, a searching and affectionate portrait of her grandparents, evinced her inclination toward narrative and characterization, as have other of her beautiful poems. *Through the Ivory Gate* was preceded by a small book of fiction titled *Fifth Sunday*. With this intelligent novel of a young black woman's coming-of-age, Dove pursues her talents in prose.

Ntozake Shange, a multi-talented writer best known for her play *for colored girls who have considered suicide/when the rainbow is enuf* and the novel *Sassafrass, Cypress & Indigo*, in her third novel, *Liliane: Resurrection of the Daughter*, also offers a daring portrait of a black woman artist re-creating herself out of social and psychological chaos, the fragmentation that haunts our time, our nation, ourselves.

Liliane is undergoing a traditional psychoanalysis. Brief dialogues headed "Room in the Dark" preface the more novelistic chapters, allowing us to eavesdrop on therapeutic sessions in which Liliane searches for a deeper understanding of her anxieties and anger, a fuller understanding of her feelings for her parents. Her task is to learn to listen to herself. As her analyst says about the panic Liliane feels as she tries to do this, "It's not really the silence you believe you can't survive. It's the noise in your head that you only hear in silence."

Daughter of Judge Parnell Lincoln, a powerful man who "kept score," and S. (for Sunday) Bliss LaFontaine Lincoln, who left the Judge to run off with a white man, Liliane is burdened by grievances she will learn to acknowledge and deal with, but as the book opens she is still finding her way in the world: "I travel a lot. I look at men and take some home or leave the country, borders have never intimidated me. My passport is in order and I carry letters of credit, perfume, four fancy dresses and six nightgowns.... I paint." She believes in "honor, color, and good sex."

There is considerable sex in this book, but there is also a love of language. Liliane describes what she sees and feels when she paints: "Women wrapped in blue-black swishes of spun cotton float through the streets. . . .I am allowing my fingers to float as the women do, over the cobblestones, reddened dirt paths, billows of dust following donkeys, mules, bicycles."

In the narrative chapters, language is often presented in monologues, voices inflected and rising off the page to reach the reader's ear as well as eye. One may think of these chapters as soliloquies, even, for there is an interesting theatricality to the book's structure, as if it could be dismantled and reassembled, like a series of stage sets. Roxie, Lollie, Bernadette—friends of Liliane from childhood—speak in turn, as do some of the lovers, each individuated voice giving us another "view" of Liliane but also enlarging the novel's historical reach, taking us from the North to the South and back again. Yet it is Liliane who is at the center and holds our attention, as she embodies and makes personal a universal struggle to overcome divisive hatreds, become whole.

White folks got us so tangled up and wound round ourselves we can't live without them or the idea of them where we can touch it. If we live like white folks don't exist, like they don't matter, they kill us. . . .If we act decent, they treat us like fools. If we spend our lives hating them, we look as foolish and psychotic as they do to the rest of the world.

Why, she wants to know, did her mother leave *her*—for it was not only her father who was left—and how could she have left her for a *white* man? As Liliane sees it, "She walks out the door, leaves me behind, goes off with her lover to start a new life, and I have to live with her over and over again, because all I had was memories. I had memories and pictures. Memories and stories I'd tell sometimes. That's all I had." Liliane's healing takes place as she begins to understand the limited choices available to her mother and that those choices need not determine hers.

A final soliloquy by Victor-Jésus, a photographer, who argues that he is "always gointa be more black" than American blacks, provides a kind of dream-resurrection, as all the characters, even the dead Sawyer and his fragile sister Hyacinthe, even poor murdered Roxie—or as Liliane says, "our friends, our ghosts, and the gods we love"—appear in the pictures he takes of Lollie's wedding. Reunited in joy with family and friends, Sunday Bliss's daughter, following her journey through history and self, has returned to a new life, or the old life newly cherished.

(But the old life had its charms, too, for the reader. Who could resist a character who says, when a certain man is not paying proper attention, "I'm not going to come out of my house until there are some hip black people in outer space"?)

In *Liliane*, Shange has written a novel that manages to be both risky and stylish. It moves fast and carries the reader into areas of sensibility not always entered. Of "memories and pictures," of "memories and stories," she has made a novel that takes its place on the shelf—by now, shelves—of exciting fiction by contemporary black women, all of whom are invaluably enlarging American literature's sense of itself.

Black women writers—all of them, mentioned above or not—bring to the rest of American literature an otherness that works to make a whole, which is to say, a definable entity, without which we simply are not one nation, much less indivisible, with freedom and liberty for all. How interesting and hopeful it is that a union is by definition a coming together, that components may remain distinct and capable of distillation while mixing to form a new compound. And incidentally, what good reading.

ART WE CANNOT LIVE WITHOUT: MARY WARD BROWN

Two published collections comprising twenty-one short stories and one memoir have been sufficient to establish Mary Ward Brown as one of contemporary southern fiction's most important writers. There simply is no one else who is covering the same ground in the same way, and it is territory essential to an understanding of the South and it is traversed intelligently, calmly, and with a truthful care for anyone she meets en route.

What is her territory? Predominantly race, class, gender, and age in a South changing from old to new. Her stories usually take place in an era that precedes the settings of Bobbie Ann Mason, Lee Smith, and Jill McCorkle—the late fifties, the sixties, and the early seventies—but reflect events, situations, and attitudes that postdate the stories of Flannery O'Connor and Eudora Welty. Black Power confronts the white establishment. White city government gives way to black. The elderly, black and white, struggle to reconcile the past with the present. A younger generation labors under the unresolved resentments and anxieties of an older.   In "A Meeting on the Road," the powerful closing story in her second book, *It Wasn't All Dancing*, Ben Neighbors, a white lawyer who has been abruptly voted out of his job as legal counsel to the County Commission, is walking out his feelings of anger when he is nearly run over by a black man who turns out to be the grandson of the black woman who raised him—and who is also likely the son of Henry Philpot, the man who was his best friend in childhood but has now returned to town and, a new member of the Commission, made the motion to fire him. Although Ben is "even-tempered by nature," when he is fired by the Commission his feelings are "like an angry crowd yelling and protesting, trying to get out." The passing car kicks up a pebble that hits him in the face. "Run over me then, God damn it!" Ben shouts.   And when the driver stops, Ben adds, "You just want to run over somebody, all of you, every chance you get! . . .Only a nigger would do something like that!"

Ben is horrified to hear himself.   "It came out of nowhere," Brown writes, "a word he despised, never used, even in jest.   He'd winced to hear it all of his life."

Indeed, Ben has spent a lifetime adapting to the changes in his town, knowing that "Ashton was a black town now. . .and whites could expect from them what they'd received in the past."   He doesn't forget that the house he lives in and loves was "built with slave labor before the Civil War."   He remembers the black woman who raised him, the driver's grandmother, Easter Agee, with affection so deep that when it surfaces, he is nearly overwhelmed.   He wants to speak about this to the grandson, who just wants to get where he's going:

> Ben fought back the impulse to tell him anyway, as in some crucial summation to a jury, what Easter had meant to him.   But things like that weren't said any more.   They were considered racist, patronizing, some kind of put-down.
>
> Also, after Henry, he couldn't help wondering how Easter had really felt about him all those years, at night on her lumpy mattress.   If her faithfulness hadn't been

three parts necessity at the time. Things had been worse
for her then than they were for him now.

Ben and the grandson consider each other "across a no man's
land of silence." The thread of violence having subsided beneath
recognition and recollection, they turn in their respective
directions. The story closes swiftly; as the grandson drives off,
"Ben raised his hand in the semblance of a wave. 'Take care,' he
called out too late, whether to the grandson or himself he didn't
know."

      This is not safe stuff. A woman writer is writing from a
man's point of view. The man's point of view is not clear even to
himself. That the blacks in Ben's life and in the town of Ashton
have quite a different point of view is made clear to the reader, but
that point of view, also, is not easily spelled out: Easter *did* make
Ben feel loved; Henry *was* a great childhood pal, the grandson is
not out to pick a fight with Ben. But Henry *did* boot Ben off the
job. It *was* Easter's job to care for Ben. The grandson is *not about*
to stand there and let Ben mouth off at him.
      Ben's family home *was* built by slaves.

      But is it really too late for Ben? Another way to look at the
ending is to say that a white man and a black man met on a road
in Alabama, faced each other in anger, discovered a connection,
kept their fists to themselves, and parted amicably.
      Then again, perhaps not. In one of her judicious instances
of description, Brown notes that as Ben and the grandson stand
facing each other "the sun reddened and glared before starting to
set. There was no sound except the lonely, drawn-out lowing of a
cow soon to be slaughtered."
      So: A dark story? A happy ending? You decide.
      Brown's stories are often like that. She slices into the narrative
quickly and decisively; explanation and exposition are kept to a
minimum; nothing is milked for melodrama; the author does not

exaggerate, bemoan, harp, hedge, or rail; characters are allowed
to be whoever they are without apology or boast from the author.
There are no sly winks at the reader, no nudges suggesting that
the reader should be feeling this or that. In fact, the stories may
be said to be Chekhovian, and Brown has publicly acknowledged
that she considers Chekhov a major influence on her work. She
may be even more stringent than Chekhov, who would tarry to
paint a sunset or loaf beside a tree. There are sunsets, and trees,
in Brown's stories, but the scenery is never permitted to run away
with the play. It may be that a certain minimalism in the telling
is how Brown keeps the whole of a short story in such beautiful
balance. What might have been florid or overwrought remains
transparent as a windowpane. The language opens a view onto
the scene.

Here, with the mention of Chekhov, might be a good place
to assert that Mary Ward Brown is not usefully thought of as
a regionalist writer, despite her family roots in Alabama and
despite her use of southern settings. That is, she is a southern
writer but not a regionalist writer. The stories are informed by
a cosmopolitan sensibility. As often as they reflect the South of
an earlier time, they reflect, too, the cultural accouterments of
present-day, educated, middle-class life. A story that makes this
clear, in *It Wasn't All Dancing*, is "Alone in a Foreign Country,"
in which the protagonist, Cathy from Mississippi, joins a group
of English teachers on a tour of Moscow. She is interested in
Russian literature but is also hoping to meet a suitable man,
"nice, literary, close to a doctorate, maybe." On her first night in
Moscow, she is given a single room at the hotel. The organizer of
the tour advises her to keep her door locked.

As she lies in bed in the darkness, her imagination begins
to get the better of her. In a laugh-out-loud sequence that many
women who have traveled solo will recognize, she mishears
noises, tries to dial 911 (in Russia), piles furniture against the
door to prevent anyone from entering, remembers every horror
story she has ever heard about rape and murder, and finally,

exhausted, falls asleep—but not before realizing that "sometime, somewhere, her time would come."

And what then? The question had prowled around her consciousness before. But safe at home, she'd shut it out.
    Would she be blotted out and simply not be? Go back to the nothingness from which she'd been born? The steady little flame that was her self would go out, and darkness would descend forever. For infinity!

In the morning, the group sets out for Chekhov's house. The group has found out about the furniture piled against Cathy's door and can't resist teasing her a little. When Cathy tries to talk seriously about death to Beverly, who has befriended her, Beverly does not want to listen. Cathy remembers that Tolstoy, too, had, on a night away from home, understood his own mortality and that it had changed his life. Disembarking from the bus, Beverly leaves Cathy behind. It seems that what Cathy has discovered has separated her from the others. Fear of death may be everybody's secret, but it is a secret not to be shared, at least not easily, and perhaps only in art—which is what Brown has accomplished in this story. It's a remarkable evocation of a young person's coming-to-awareness of the human condition.

A story similar in its ability to locate the universal in the personal is "The Amaryllis," from Ward's first collection, *Tongues of Flame.* Judge Manderville, whose wife has recently died, has been given an amaryllis bulb by his daughter-in-law, Mary Ann. With fascination and delight, he has watched it grow, this flower "so beautiful it had come to dominate the entire house. It was not only alive but dramatically alive" and when the flower is at its most beautiful, he realizes he has to share it. The question is, With whom? He wishes his Margaret were present to enjoy it with him.

He knows that his son and daughter-in-law care about him, but they lead busy lives that do not leave room for visiting an elderly widower on the spur of the moment. He tries to think of friends he might call. Meanwhile, his friend McGowan is alone on his birthday, and the Judge invites himself over for a late-afternoon coffee, taking a birthday cake with him. After the little celebration, he returns home to gaze again at the amaryllis:

> Looking at the blooms, he thought of words like *pure* and *noble*, and old lines of poetry like "Euclid alone has looked on *Beauty bare.*"
> In return, the plant seemed neither friendly nor unfriendly. It was simply there in all its glory, however fleeting. It was the fleetingness, he thought, that put on the pressure.

The next day, with both blooms "exud[ing] a kind of concentrated freshness like early morning in the woods, a baby's skin, or eyes just waking from sleep," he decides to hold an open house for the fully opened flower. He wants to show it to folks who will appreciate it. He leaves a note asking the postman to come in the house. McGowen will have lunch with him and hang around for the rest of the day. It is a Friday, which means Pot, who used to cook and clean for the Judge and his wife fulltime, will be there to help. The Judge and Pot have been together for a long time and Pot, too, has lost his wife. They stayed friendly during the civil rights conflict, and now, when Pot "looked at the flower with what it deserved, reverence," the Judge felt "a surge of love" for him.

The event is quite successful, with Pot pouring coffee and McGowan helping the conversation to flow. One woman mentions the Judge's late wife, saying she had been "lovely," and tears spring to his eyes, but the party is about the amaryllis, or, as McGowan says, "the big petunia—or whatever the hell its name is," and the mood is lively and happy. The Judge's son calls to say he'll bring the wife and kids for an overnight stay in a couple of weeks.

But the day after the party, the Judge looks at the amaryllis and wonders, "[W]ere the blooms quite as fresh, really as perfect, as yesterday? . . .The first blooms passed their prime and began to age in the same way that people did, the Judge thought." Each successive day, the amaryllis is less what it was, and the Judge loses interest in it, although the feeling shames him a bit.

Another writer might have ended the story here, with the Judge removing the shot plant from the room, its beauty evanescent and gone. The Judge moves the plant into the pantry before his son's visit; it is not worth remarking anymore. But, someone tells him, a year from now he will be able to revive it. A little TLC, and "the amaryllis would grow and bloom again. It seemed incredible, but all the gardeners and flower people assured him it was true."

Love, the fragility of it and of the beloved, loss, age, loneliness, the nature of community and how it can rescue, friendship as something done and not just declared, reverence for beauty, for what is perfect—the story is about all these, but perhaps it is most of all about our human capacity to recover from disappointment and despair, again and again as needed, to hold in our hearts the knowledge that the transitory may return whether we recognize it or are present for it or not, or even if the return eventuates in some place we do not yet know.

How does Brown do it? First of all, as suggested earlier, economically. Her beginnings place us inside the narratives without preamble. Here is the first paragraph of "New Dresses" (*Tongues of Flame*):

Mrs. Lovelady, in a morning-fresh white uniform, helped Lisa's mother-in-law, Mrs. Worthy, into the car. Lisa could only stand by and watch. The bucket seat was too low and dangerously tilted for Mrs. Worthy as she was now, and Lisa wished she had listened to David, had come in his car instead of her own as he'd tried to tell her. Mrs. Lovelady kept smiling, for Mrs. Worthy's sake. Her eyes froze over when she looked at Lisa.

Something is happening in the first sentence. And speaking of sentences, is it possible to pack more information into five such un-Faulknerian sentences? We know that Mrs. Worth is old and frail, that her nurse disapproves of Mrs. Worthy's daughter-in-law, that the daughter-in-law and Mrs. Worthy's son are still jostling for space and control in their marriage. We see the sporty car and the old lady, the young woman, and the nurse in her white uniform that smells like morning. We even see the son's car that is not there.

Hewing to the line of the narrative, her stories say what they need to say and no more, achieving their ends without detour or distraction. It is as if the stories know there is only one way to travel from beginning to end—the right way, as it turns out—and consequently, they convey a sense of surety to the reader, who, feeling herself to be in good hands, can give herself over to the act of reading. This has always seemed to me one of the best gifts a writer can offer to a reader. The reader gets to enter the story as if it were a house—another *open house*—and live there for the duration. It seems to me an act of kindness, one that can't be performed by a writer too anxious to allow the reader her own response to what she finds.

Let's look again at the author's voice, which "does not exaggerate, bemoan, harp, hedge, or rail." It is a voice that makes the reader feel at home and at ease. A reasonable, reasoned voice. Even when the story pinches a nerve or refers to the ineffable—physical pain and spiritual pleasure both being essentially private—the voice of the story remains measured and calm. A woman whose husband cheated on her with a mistress when he was alive—and who had actually told her, one night when she inched closer to him in bed, "Go to sleep. . . .You're too bony for me"—reaches a point where she feels confident that the universe has been morally ordered and "[b]eyond, in mystic clarity, lay endless vistas of shimmering peace" ("Good-bye, Cliff," *Tongues of Flame*). We believe that she believes, whether or not we believe in "mystic clarity." When Sally, in "Let Him Live" (*Tongues of Flame*), rises after falling asleep during the prayer chain, we have no trouble accepting that "one foot was numb," that "[h]er mouth tasted of dissipation," that "[t]he church had a close waxy smell," and we can recall what it is like to have pins and needles in a cramped foot, a dry, stale feeling in our mouth. In "Disturber of the Peace" (*Tongues of Flame*), Jeannette, having been jilted by her fiancé, Frank, for another woman, and become involved, on the rebound, with the married and lonely and woebegone Dr. Wells, finds a tall cross, lit by light bulbs, has been placed in the churchyard across the street from her apartment, whence it shines "as if a huge outdoor spotlight were fixed on her bed." The result of the stories' temperate, even dispassionate, voice is that the reader can form her own response, her own take on the situation, free of authorial interference. Even more important, the reader can experience the narrative as she will, without feeling there is a certain way she is *supposed* to react. There are not many writers who respect their readers sufficiently to do this. Mary Ward Brown does. Asked in an interview for *First Draft*, "[W]hat do you think your stories teach us about the meaning of life?", she answered, "I don't think my stories add up to any conclusions about life. . . .What they do add up to is its importance—human life, its importance."

Without making value judgments about them, then, Brown retires from the stage, leaving it to her characters. They act on their own. "I don't start out with a story," she told *Southern Living* in August 1988. "I discover it. And the characters begin to live. They do. They finish it. I will just be whatever character is in the scene. And how would I feel? What would I say if I were that character?" In *It Wasn't All Dancing*'s "No Sound in the Night," her characters include Jean Goodwyn, the new editor of the local paper; her boyfriend, Bob Carter, who works for his father's insurance company as a salesman; and Ed, Henshaw, and Bunny, the newspaper's linotypist, ad man, and printer's devil, in that order. Bunny—who looks a bit rabbity and is thirty-two and mentally challenged—is surprised and pleased to find that "Jean treated him just like she did Ed and Henshaw." Soon he is well nigh lovestruck, but too polite and shy to let Jean know that. Besides, there's that boyfriend.

The boyfriend, however, is annoyed by Jean's long hours at work, her sudden departures to interview sources and track down stories. As her editorials begin to receive attention, his impatience increases. Bunny overhears the boyfriend making a date with another girl.

> Bunny didn't use bad words. They were for grown men not boys. In spite of his age he knew he was less man than boy. "Like a child," he'd heard people say when they talked about him. But hurrying back to the shop with Jean's sandwich and milk shake, he kept saying over and over, son of a bitch, that son of a bitch. He didn't know he was saying it out loud until he heard his own voice.

Jean quietly removes her engagement ring. She grows sad and thin and silent.

> Bunny's heart ached to look at her and, longing to comfort her, he recognized at last the yearning that had plagued him for weeks. He wanted to touch her.

But Bunny won't; he doesn't dare. He remembers liking a girl in elementary school, and that he thought she liked him back until he attempted to kiss her. The girl looked at him with such distaste that he turned and fled.

The boyfriend marries and it is public knowledge. Jean puts the rejection behind her and throws herself into her work. Knowing she is going to be late at the office, Bunny changes into clean clothes and combs his hair, though he "never really looked at his face in the mirror. Not once did he meet the eyes fringed with pale, rabbity lashes," and rushes out to see her.

And how will she react when she sees him? He imagines her shock, her revulsion, and he turns and flees. "His footsteps on the sidewalk made no sound in the night."

In Chekhov's story "The Kiss," the timid, unprepossessing, and socially inexperienced Staff-Captain Ryabovich, entering a dark room during a party, is kissed accidentally, apparently mistaken for an awaited lover. Although his emotions differ from Bunny's—Ryabovich is at first elated, then curious as to which of the women might have kissed him, then dissatisfied with the possibilities; later, he daydreams of marriage, of a family and children; and later still, when he and two batteries return to the village in which the party had taken place and it appears there will be no party this time, he loses hope—when at last an invitation for a second visit does arrive, he refuses to go, ensuring that he will remain forever lonely. He cuts off his nose to spite his face. Bunny is not as vain or as self-deluded as Ryabovich, and Ryabovich undergoes a more complex series of feelings than Bunny does, but both stories are masterful studies of men who have learned not to act upon their desires; both stories are utterly unsentimental; and both stories are deeply saddening.

"No Sound in the Night" takes us into the heart of one of the overlooked in our world, a man whose life is largely written off by others, who is noticed, if at all, only as someone without a future. He is expected to stay on the sidelines; he has been benched by life, and he is not supposed to complain about it nor step onto the playing field. But that doesn't mean his heart is not breaking; that doesn't mean it hasn't been breaking all along, for years, ever since the little girl recoiled from him.

At the same time we know that Jean is a caring, straight-forward, serious young lady, that she is by nature friendly and democratic, and that she has not led Bunny on and, even though she would probably not consider him a likely replacement for her erstwhile boyfriend, she probably would not be aghast. She would find some unhurtful way to explain the situation. Partly, we want to say to Bunny, Go for it!, and partly, we are relieved that he does not. The tension between the two wishes is like a taut wire vibrating: the painful poignance of the story reverberates for a long time.

Their devotion to character guides Chekhov and Brown safely past the pitfall of sentimentality, on the lip of which so many otherwise promising narratives have teetered before plunging into obscurity. (I will just say here that sentimentality in literature has nothing to do with happy endings, and everything to do with falsehood and inaccuracy.) "Fruit of the Season" (*Tongues of Flame*) tracks three black children, Cato, Daisy, and Jones, as they set out by themselves to pick berries. They are the offspring of Bessie Lee, cook to Mrs. Frances Marshall, whose husband is a landowner in Alabama in 1959. The children are picking dewberries—Bessie calls them "jewberries"—on the Jackson property, and Bessie has told them to pick some for Mrs. Marshall.

The children are marvelously depicted, all the way down to ten-year-old Cato's "battered felt hat cut full of diamond-shaped air holes" and Jones's childishness when, "bored with berries, he began finding things to put in his bucket. Leaves, grass, a dead grasshopper, and live crickets." Equally vivid are the hot, sticky day, the hard work, the buckets becoming heavier and heavier.

Think of all the places three kids, on their own on a stifling day, might go in a story. Think of what storylines might be developed. Think of the sweet, adorable, touching scenes waiting in the margin.

What happens is that, arriving with their buckets of berries at Mrs. Marshall's house, "Cato thought of his own hot little house and of the blackness he would never outgrow. . . .When he turned to the bucket on the ground, his eyes seemed to darken. Without a word, he gathered up the saliva in his mouth, leaned over, and spit on the berries." Daisy does it, too, and then the children are spitting and laughing, making a game out of it.

They knock on the door, offering the berries to Mrs. Jackson. The berries are not for sale, they say, hoping for glasses of lemonade in return for their gift. But Frances Marshall knows that there is a price attached, whether she pays in money or not. If she doesn't give them money, she will have to find ways to thank them, ways that go beyond cool drinks and cookies and that while she is sharing her largess, Bessie Lee and the other

blacks on the place are attending "secret race meetings at night."
Life in the South is changing.

Frances tells them she will pay for the berries. She smiles,
gives Cato a dollar bill, and then she "opened the door to let them
out."

This story, with its smiling rage, smoulders; we feel that what
doesn't erupt now will erupt later, a volcano of resentment spilling
over into hatred. And who will win? The children think they
have fixed Mrs. Marshall good, but what have they gotten by it?
Frances Marshall thinks she has outwitted the children, but she
can't begin to imagine what they've done. "Fruit of the Season"
is a brilliant short story, driven by Brown's talent for divining the
truth—the truth of each character—and telling it straight. The
title itself, appearing so innocent and fresh at the story's start, in
retrospect takes on a sinister, more extreme coloration, echoing
the poem sung by Billie Holiday as "Strange Fruit."

Mary Ward Brown grew up in Hamburg, Alabama, near
Selma, and still lives in her childhood home, which was passed
on to her at her father's death. She began publishing in the
fifties, but gave it up, gave writing up as well, feeling a need to
dedicate herself to her roles as wife and mother. She has said
that she could not be content writing fiction if she couldn't give
it "everything I had." Years later, when she did have the time
and solitude to do it, she returned to writing. *Tongues of Flame*
won the PEN/Hemingway Award for first fiction, the Lillian
Smith Award, and the Alabama Library Association Award.
The author received the Harper Lee Award in 2002, with the
publication of *It Wasn't All Dancing*, and the Hillsdale Prize for
Fiction from the Fellowship of Southern Writers in 2003. The
strength of spirit that supported her in her decisions, first, to
put her writing on hold while she attended to family and farm,
and second, to return to writing when the time came, must be
also the source of her compassionate deference to character:
not every writer would be capable of the choices she made. She
is so good at letting others take center stage that her memoir,

"Swing Low," presented as the central, pivotal piece in *It Wasn't All Dancing*, turns out to be not about her but about her mother and her mother's lifelong friendship with a black man named William Edwards.

Edwards was the house cleaner in the Ward household, with Mary Ward Brown's mother as his boss, "though in a way they were workers together, since they had the same lord and master, my father. My mother called my father Mister Ward...." Running the commissary as well as the household, Brown's mother toiled long, hard hours, often made harder by her helper's alcoholic inclinations. Then again, those hours were often made more bearable by his comradely conversation. As Mister Ward's farm expanded to include "a cotton gin, saw mill, planer mill, grist mill, blacksmith shop, beef cattle and dairy, besides all the crops" and "[m]ore than two hundred black people lived and worked on the place," Brown's mother and William Edwards became old buddies. When Mister Ward discovers someone has been hitting his own bottle of booze and making off with small items and then cash, the thief turns out to be Edwards, who, now a widower, is frantically trying to hold the interest of a selfish young woman. Brown's mother tries to cover for him. Mister Ward is not fooled, but he does not discharge Edwards, whose woman has left him for somebody else. Edwards gives up drinking for good. But Brown's mother is failing; examinations and tests and treatments have come too late to save her from a progressing cancer. "[N]ow it was her turn to lean on someone, and she leaned most on William, who was always there." Her final words are "Poor William. Don't cry..." But William does cry.

Humorous and heartbreaking, "Swing Low" informs us not only about the world in which Mary Ward Brown was raised but also about herself; we find out that she was always absorbed in noticing the Other—the self who is not oneself. That is the essential personal trait of a serious fiction writer. Mary Ward Brown is serious. She has said that she hopes, with her writing, to create "a piece of art you can live with, like a beautiful object," but because she hazards minefields to bring home the truth, what she has created is art we cannot live without.

A GIRL IN A LIBRARY

To be both young and wanting to be a writer is to experience a form of unrequited love. The young writer's relation to the object of her desire is all in the subjunctive: *I wish! If only!* And, *Were something—this, that—to happen!* And, *If someone, if I, should happen to!* And most of all, *If only I could, I would!* In my seventeenth year I solemnly swore, in a spiral notebook, to *quit* writing until after I'd managed to become something else: a scientist or a philosopher. But love returns, each new man wearing the same old face you always fell for, and when I finally heard from a friend, a few years later, that there were schools where you could actually earn academic credit for indulging your passion, my heart leapt, and I sent off for their college catalogues.

In those days, there were three schools—or three I knew of—granting MFAs in creative writing. Stanford, in California, was on the other side of the moon. The Iowa Writers Workshop wanted transcripts from every college you'd attended, and since not even counting graduate school I'd made six transfers to five colleges and had gotten kicked out of two, there was, I thought, no point in applying to the Iowa Writers Workshop.

Finally there was the University of North Carolina at Greensboro, which had just started a graduate program in creative writing. "Here," my informant told me, "read this." He handed me a volume of poetry titled *Paper Horse* by someone named Robert Watson. The program put a toe in the water with three students in 1963 before it took the plunge the following year with the first official and full-size class. In September, 1965, I arrived in Greensboro with that book of poems—which had the most wonderful and audacious rhyming I'd seen in contemporary poetry—safely packed in the footlocker my father had stowed in the trunk of the car.

Rhyme remakes the world in harmony. "All quarrels turn to song," the poet had written in a poem called "Watson on the Beach":

> Sounds fill me until only sound exists—
> Sound sun and stars once made,
> And light recorded on our sea
> Is now replayed from water's memory,
> Record of our seed in sound,
> Around, around,
> World lost, world found.

Here was a poet unafraid to rhyme out in the open, not hiding behind slant or half rhymes. He carried it off by cutting lusciously full rhymes with the sharp vinegar of unexpected placement. But he was not, it turned out, teaching the poetry workshop that semester. I was heartbroken until he agreed to do a playwriting tutorial with me. I was also to have the privilege of copy editing his forthcoming book of poetry, *Advantages of Dark*. If ever a student had a happier apprenticeship, I don't know who or when.

The poetry workshop was going to be taught by a young fellow named Fred Chappell. If Watson's work offered a long-sought-for validation, Chappell's was a challenge I raced to meet. The first time I met him I knew he would change my life as a writer. I felt that there were correspondences in what we wanted to accomplish in art and that he would be a model for me. Perhaps I was a little afraid of failing his expectations—though I doubt he had any other than those I projected onto him. My sense of it was that here was someone who would be disappointed, and probably bored, too, by anything less than a poetry carved out of bone.

After registering for classes, I returned to the dorm to see my parents off on the drive back to Richmond. They were in the front seat of the car, gunning the motor under a shade tree, when Chappell came strolling across the lawn. I introduced him to them, they exchanged a few words, and he continued on his way, not knowing that both my parents adored him on sight and asked if they could please adopt him.

That first semester, Chappell's pedagogical philosophy was to be as fierce as possible in his criticism. If we could take it, the philosophy went, we might become writers. I think I *developed* the technique Holly Hunter later hit on in *Broadcast News*: The class met once a week, at night, and afterwards, Chappell and some of the students would gather at the Pickwick, a local hangout. Every week, right after class, I disappeared into the ladies' room in McIver and sat on the floor and cried for approximately twenty minutes; then, with that out of my system, I beat it down to the Pickwick because I did not want to miss a single word that might ever come out of Fred Chappell's mouth. What I didn't know, of course, was that this was Chappell's first graduate workshop, and he was, he told me later, scared to death. He learned to moderate his criticism, but I wouldn't trade that baptism of fire for anything.

Not so often in the Pickwick, preferring to take long walks around the city alone, was Watson. At least, this was the image we students had of him, a marvelously romantic image of the poet lost in language, finding himself on unknown street corners with a line, a metaphor, even an entire stanza as a sudden companion. "Going Nowhere Alone at Night" is the title of one of Watson's poems. We didn't know, at first, that the reason he did not frequent the Pickwick was that he was allergic to beer. Among those who did sometimes turn up in the Pickwick was my classmate William Pitt Root, who has since published many books of poetry and taught for many years at Hunter College in New York, though he escaped often to the western spaces that lend his work a Robinson Jeffers strength and now lives in Colorado. Bill was in a hurry to publish; he was sending his work out regularly when the rest of us were still figuring out that there was a professional bridge to cross between writing a book and having it appear on a library shelf. One of the poems he published in the first issue of *The Greensboro Review* had already appeared halfway across the country, in the *Beloit Poetry Journal*: Describing the renewal of spring after a fire has destroyed a church, he sees that "charred / twigs kink toward the church's shell / while blossoms nod like innocents near hell." Pretty powerful stuff for a guy of about twenty-four.

That first issue of *The Greensboro Review* was edited by Shorty Reynolds, known in more formal circles as Lawrence Judson Reynolds. *The Greensboro Review* debuted in May 1966. Shorty, who was tall and sported a goatee, said to me, "I have some bad news to break to you. We got your name backwards in the Table of Contents." I didn't care. The poems were there!

The issue had been assembled in a small but splendid building, with desks and a reading room, that was reserved for the writing students. On the top floor, up some rickety steps, was the only private office, which Bill Root had somehow snagged for himself. The building was called The Fish Bowl—because it had so many windows—and one night a faint tapping on one of the windows brought to the students' attention the renowned and later Pulitzer Prize-winning fictionist Peter Taylor, who proceeded, in tweed jacket with leather elbow patches, and wearing a tie, to climb into the room over the sill. We students naturally tried to act as though renowned fictionists were always dropping in on us through the windows.

Also represented in that issue was Harry Humes, a poet whose sense of his Appalachian heritage has stayed with him and deepened through several books of verse that is simultaneously lyrical and as unsentimental as weather. "Zero's precision coats the day," he says in a poem in the book *Winter Weeds*. "Near the center, / the air's a hawk's eye. / The season's grain stiffens. / I listen for what's there: / a freeze of blue syllables, / a hiss like deep water."

Less lyrically, but nostalgically anyway, Harry remembers getting spectacularly drunk at Taylor's house during a party whose distinguished guest of honor was Eudora Welty and throwing up, being carried home by classmates, and waking up mortified the next day. He was positive that he would never dare show his face again. He would have to leave Greensboro. He would have to have plastic surgery and sign up with the Witness Protection Program. Before he could put this plan into action, Peter Taylor showed up at his door and invited him to the Pickwick. There, Taylor comforted him by confessing that he had had a similar experience. "I once threw up," said Peter Taylor, "in Robert Penn Warren's rumble seat."

Despite parties and the Pickwick, what we were mostly doing was writing. We lived, all of us, in a haze of drafts, jazzed on coffee, competing with and applauding one another, hiding out in the library stacks, shocked into specific ambition or stunned into silence by visiting writers such as Guy Owen, Stanley Kunitz, X. J. Kennedy, Carolyn Kizer, and, certainly, Welty. Allen Tate came to teach for a while, and in his poetry class I learned to go back to the beginning and write in forms, my previous attempts at form having been erratic and unedited. I audited the lecture course in Modern Poetry, taught by Randall Jarrell and, after Jarrell's death, by Fred Chappell. Meanwhile, in those stacks, where one could make secret discoveries that didn't have to be shared in a classroom, I found Akhmatova, Borges, Berryman. I found Flaubert. I spent hours at a library table, poring over Virgil and Homer. In his lovely poem "A Girl in a Library," Jarrell, contemplating a student with her "shoes off" and her legs "curl[ed] up," imagines that her pragmatic temperament leaves little room for sensibility: ". . .with what yawns the unwilling / Flesh puts on its spirit, O my sister!" he cries, mocking her, and himself too, a bit, I think. And if he condescends in saying "I am a thought of yours: and yet, you do not think. . . ," a girl in a library, any girl in any library, may someday reply, "I was thinking so hard that you *were* a thought of mine, and when I went to write you down, you melded into a place and time that seems, now, as hard to grasp as a dream."

Students did not know that Jarrell was in the difficult last months of his life. Had I known I might not have approached him after class to ask a question. He dismissed my question as trivial, and as soon as he did, I realized that it was, but the dismissal hurt anyway. I can see now that I was probably trying to show off, to prove that I was not like his "girl in a library," and thoroughly deserved to be dismissed.

I hadn't the courage to sign up for Peter Taylor's class in fiction writing. Taylor was famous, which was scary enough, but even scarier was his southern gentlemanliness, which, I thought, might cause him to disapprove of someone whose work was not very ladylike. (I had not yet heard about Robert Penn Warren's rumble seat, or I might not have fretted about this.) But I wrote a story and showed it to Chappell, and Chappell took it to Taylor, and Taylor commented helpfully to Chappell, who conveyed the comments to me, and in this way I made enough progress with fiction so that my second year I did enroll in the fiction workshop—which was now being taught by Chappell. I had tried writing fiction before—and plays—but I considered myself primarily a poet. It may have been Watson's dramatic monologues—which so many of his poems are—that partly inspired me to undertake a poetic sequence that was essentially a narrative in lyric moments, or maybe the sequence appeared simply because I had always thought the creation of a distinct and memorable character was one of the glorious tasks any writer would want to set her shoulder to. Chappell encouraged me to explore that interest in character via fiction as well as poetry. Both Watson and Chappell moved back and forth between the genres. Jarrell had also written essays that remain unsurpassed exemplars of the form. That a writer would naturally want to tackle more than one genre was a working assumption in

Greensboro, whereas at the Iowa Writers Workshop students were being streamlined into this genre or that. It may be a smarter career move to stick to one thing, but it must be a much duller writing life. The world, in Greensboro as anywhere, is too large to be contained in a single form. The problem is not the world so much as it is the writer: to encompass all of it, the writer has to be able to know all of it, but *what* the writer can know of the world is dependent on *how* the writer knows the world—that is, the form through which she perceives it.

In fiction, the writer has a way to observe the world of relations, how one consciousness interacts with another. Mores and emotion take precedence. In essay, the writer discovers the path her own mind takes to pursue a thought: no matter the essay's subject, what the essay reveals is the mind of the writer. And in poetry, the writer encounters what C. S. Peirce called the "brute reality" of things, their thingness, their being-there. Perhaps we might have expected poetry to lead more directly to the emotions, as fiction does, but no: metaphor, while giving us the terms from which we deduce whatever it is a metaphor for, even before we can draw that deduction reminds us of the prior existence of the referents of those terms. In his poem "Proposition IVa."—a poem I love—Chappell argues, "Our senses perceive only modes, but our intellects / perceive the attributes of the flower." But our intellects, too, perceive the modes, construing the flower as if it were a sentence in a foreign language, parsing it into petal, stem, pistil and stamen. And color, fragrance, shape, and texture, even the barest auditory ripple as a breeze blows over a lilac bush are tenses in a cognitive language. In another poem, which is titled "Ideally Grasping the Actual Flower," Chappell deconstructs Kantian metaphysics and in the process converts a rose into a kind of "angel," an "Angel whose qualities / Are mathematic as a snowflake." Yet we observe, taste, feel that snowflake even before we admire its complex geometry of coldness, whiteness, softness. Then he concludes, twisting the poem's contradictions one notch further, "This truth comes to him as clear and poignant / As one's own porch light seen from a distant planet." Who won't see that small, steady light, that porch leading to the house in which one's own life has been, is being, lived, the reaching landscape, the aerial view of our vulnerable planet? Poetic language gives us the world as object, a thing we now perceive, after the word, as present to our senses. (By poetic language I mean lyric language, as epic poetry is arguably a sort of fiction.)

In other words, fiction lays bare a world of behavior; essay establishes a new intimacy with the world of mind; and poetry will lead you to objects of such vividness and immediacy that they will seem to sing to you. And perhaps they are singing to you, and perhaps you will be unable to sail on but will stay there, among the sirens, ravished and a little insane, as long as you live.

These are not absolute distinctions, but there is enough truth in them to make a writer want to work in all the forms, writing poetry poetically, fiction fictionally, and essay essayistically. Again, if anyone's interested in broad generalizations, I might say that this means, in poetry, a heightened awareness of line; in essay, a heightened awareness of the paragraph; in short story, a heightened awareness of the sentence, or voice; and in the novel, a heightened awareness of scene.

Our teachers had different methods of heightening our awareness. Chappell's was to show us, in each piece submitted by a student, how that piece might realize itself. He had an extraordinary knack for helping students to discover what was already, given the evidence of the work, on their minds. He was not cloning himself, as some writing teachers I've met elsewhere must be said to do. Watson's method was even more indirect, at least in the tutorials I had with him: he didn't so much criticize as carry on a conversation in art by responding to submitted work with work of his own, which then, of course, prompted more work. Tate's method appeared to be direct, but was not: he handed out actual assignments, obliging us to write in specific forms, but his attention to the requirements of those forms was so strict that we were less sensible of his own tastes than of the tradition. For example, he wouldn't allow us to rhyme a plural with a singular, something I can't do to this day without a tiny twinge of shame, as if I were splitting an infinitive. He'd flick his gold cigarette lighter open and shut, perhaps draw a hand across his high brow, and with the patience of Job explain, one more time, that forms not followed were not forms.

A note, now, about wives. By the time I took Tate's poetry workshop I had finished my degree and had married Jonathan Silver, a visiting lecturer in the Art Department, thereby becoming one of the wives. It was an impressive group to belong to: it included Betty Watson, already a painter of national repute; Eleanor Ross Taylor, an author of complex and ambitious poems; Sue Chappell, who was boldly finishing a degree even while being a faculty wife; Judith Root, who was quietly writing her own witty, urbane poetry while letting Bill be the front runner; Bertha Harris, an ex-wife but with a child and a contract (and in those pre-literary-careerist days, it was a woman writer's being strong enough to be a single mother, not her having a contract, that knocked us out); and others. We wanted to do our work, but we also wanted to participate in life. Randall Jarrell liked to wrap his arm around Mary's so they could toast each other, clinking glasses in restaurants while their faces were close, each looking into the other's eyes. It was Eleanor Taylor who, at my engagement party, took Jonathan aside and said, "You are marrying a writer. You must not ask her to do the dishes." This good advice, alas, he forgot within a week of the wedding. That marriage, which yanked out my heart and gave it to me to carry everywhere, a weight, a liability, a helpless child, was over in three years, though I was still holding my heart in my hands. Advice helps, but not enough.

It was not only the wives who had marital advice to offer: passing the perambulating Watson on the street one day early in my marriage to Jonathan, I admitted that I didn't know how to cook. "Oh," he said, "cooking's simple. First you buy a chicken. Then you boil it in some water. Just be sure to add vodka to the water."

And that's the recipe for Bob Watson's Boiled Chicken.

The soundtrack for all these adventures was—what else— The Beatles. Not that this was a retreating Age of Innocence: the news of the war was part of the daily buzz in the student union; the struggle for an integrated society was at least as much on

students' and teachers' minds as literature, and seemed to some
of us not unrelated to the problems of language. Women were
still very much limited by notions of who and what they ought
to be, but they were beginning to defy prescriptive definitions in
a search for self that would lead to a fight for the right to be that
self, and in Greensboro, where no one was looking, where the
days could lapse in a fever dream of hard work and excited idea,
we began, the women and the men of what was then a new kind
of community, a community of creativity, to be our truest selves,
not, now, sighingly hypothetical or prospective, for in art one is no
longer contingent on circumstance. One makes circumstance.

TWO FEUILLETONS, EACH MANAGING TO MENTION EMILY DICKINSON

LOCATING THE FEMALE SELF IN RELATION TO THE MALE TRADITION

I used to think all writers were male, even the female ones. If a writer wrote well, it meant she had a man's way of thinking, a man's way of feeling, a breadth and depth found more often among men than women. Women bore children, but a man could contain multitudes. Women kept the home-fires burning, but a man could join the army and see the world while Penelope wove and unraveled, wove and unraveled, and waited and waited. Women were conservative, men creative. So obviously, if a woman did write well, it was because she was a man.

I subscribed to these notions because, for one thing, whenever my older brother asked me to name a great woman composer, a great woman mathematician, a great woman philosopher, I was stumped, and for another, I was still in the seventh grade and hadn't yet read much writing by women. I couldn't, however, quite think of *myself* as a male writer—or at least, I didn't see how I could and still have a crush on Earl Tanner, the class clown who sat three rows to the left of me and who, I was convinced, was a misunderstood genius. It was so *unfair* that he kept getting sent to the principal's office.

This task of locating a female self in relation to a male tradition is not insignificant, though some male writers and even some female writers think so. It exists even when the female writer is fortunate, as I was, to find generous, encouraging male friends and mentors. George Garrett, Henry Taylor, R. H. W. Dillard, Fred Chappell, Abraham Rothberg, and David R. Slavitt were among those who made me feel welcome in the ever ongoing community of writers.

But it is a lot for a young girl to deal with: how does she resolve the paradox of identifying with, sympathizing with, passionately admiring the words of men and at the same time feeling her own experience and perspective and the lives of her sisters everywhere, those who came before her and those on the planet now, have been ignored or distorted or abridged in literature? She can find herself becoming confused. She can find herself hoping that boyfriends will tell her that she "thinks like a man" and that critics will write that she's cute. Maybe I should have looked to Emily Dickinson, but Emily Dickinson was male, at least when compared with Edna St. Vincent Millay, who seemed to be the only alternative, one with whom I felt no affinity. It was a help to me, in the early sixties, to discover Akhmatova's poetry in the library stacks. (But a man said to me, "I don't find her very interesting.") Earlier, I had stumbled on a book by H.D. in Mincer's Pipe Shop in Charlottesville (where another man, glancing at the cover, said, "Thin stuff.") And pretty soon, for me, there were Rich, Sexton, Plath, Kizer, and Bishop, to mention a few, some of them actually brought to my attention by men, and at last the seventies introduced many contemporary women poets to the world, and the women's movement enlightened us all regarding women poets in history. The anthology *One Hundred Great Poems*, edited by Carolyn Kizer, is a marvelous summation of that history.

Mostly, though, what I did all those years was argue with the male poets as I read them. "Argue" may be too strong a word.

These were not shouting matches. My confutations were written responses, and the act of writing them was a dialogue not only with the masculine antecedent but with my own self, an attempt to figure out how, exactly, *I* felt, *I* thought, since it would be pointless, in my opinion, to rant and rave (things women poets were sometimes, and sometimes wrongly, accused of doing). That would be the *reacting* of writing, not the act of writing. A mostly male tradition obliged me to think long and hard about all kinds of matters, from gender to love to justice to time and death and more, and for this I am—a woman would have to be a fool not to be—grateful.

A GRACE BEYOND THE REACH OF ART: TEACHING POETRY

How might the idea of grace come together with the idea of academia? I teach at the University of Wisconsin in Madison. UW is a huge bureaucracy, and surely nobody ever got "bureaucracy" and "grace" into the same sentence. It's true that in my time at UW I've known a dean or two who plainly expected to be addressed as "Your Grace," but presumably that's not exactly the answer this question anticipates.

Do I feel graceful or gracious when I teach? No. I usually feel like I should have had a second cup of coffee before I came to class. Do I feel I'm a conduit for poetry's saving grace, a kind of priest conferring poetic blessings upon my students? I wish!

In spite of their early-morning grogginess, in spite of—if they are budding writers or scholars—their egos, and—if we are in the Humanities Building—in spite of the lack of even one window, my students do sometimes receive a blessing of poetry, a bloom of benediction showing in their flushed, surprised, and pleased faces, but the poems do that, not me.

The legend of the Humanities Building, by the way, is that it is as ugly as it is because the contractor misread the blueprints and built it wrong side out. They say that the architect, upon seeing the result, hanged himself. This is easy to believe, because it's what we all feel we want to do after several hours in a room with no window and with fluorescent lights buzzing a lot worse than any fly Emily Dickinson ever heard.

Of course it is the students, each of them, whose presence alchemizes pedagogy into grace, so that the hapless professor, meaning me, you understand, can see a poem or the world in a new, lighted way, receive a vision of the possible. Maria, writing poems that practically ooze an enviable sensuality and playfulness, intense Meg, always achingly anxious and therefore ever precise and powerful in her lyrics, or brilliant—that says it all—Erin brings me a piece of shaped language that lifts me out of my frowning or scowling or, anyway, insufficiently caffeinated self. In my lit class, a student, a sorority pledge with long, lazy limbs that she stretches unself-consciously, says, "My college life up to now has been about drinking and socializing, and my friends thought I was crazy to sign up for this, but you know what? I'm discovering that I love reading poetry! And I'm beginning to believe I'm *good* at reading poetry!"

Now *that's* a benediction. That's when my face starts to flush, as I am surprised by joy.

My friend was a woman writer, as I am, but younger. We walked back together from lunch at a local restaurant to our respective houses, which were only a block apart—much less distance to traverse, I suddenly realized, than the generation gap.

She had just said, "I think we all have to live in such a way as to avoid regret. We simply have to make up our minds not to be seduced into bitterness."

What brought this on? I had been telling her about another friend of mine, a writer *older* than I, who believed no one wanted to read her work anymore. This older woman had had a long and distinguished career but—or so she believed—publishers felt she had lost touch with the contemporary scene.

"That's not always easy to do," I replied, troubled by what seemed to me a lack of awareness of life's contingencies. "Not everyone is so lucky." I did not say "as you," because most people hate to have their success attributed to luck, but I thought she might be able to understand the role *bad* luck plays in so-called unsuccessful lives.

She was so young, so confident. She was swinging her arms as we walked, and the sunlight made little diamond panes on her sunglasses, as if she were wearing Tiffany shades. She said, "We choose how we live, and we can choose to live in ways we won't feel sour about later."

Part of me wished that she were right. But we are not gods, only human beings, and it is human to feel regret for things you have done and wish you had not, for things you have not and wish you had, for opportunities missed or bungled or never offered. It is also human, as someone noted, to err. Whose choices are never wrong?

As we walked—past the two-story frame houses, the children running squealing through a lawn sprinkler, a college girl sunning herself in cut-offs on a lounge chair dragged out to the driveway—I remembered my own regrets. Perhaps, it occurred to me, the majority of my regrets could be boiled down to one big regret: I regretted not having had any self-esteem for so long. After all, self-esteem is surely our best inoculation against doing stupid things—things one might one day *regret*. But not even self-esteem makes for immunity to chance and circumstance. Not even self-esteem can make us, or those we love, immortal.

Could this young woman escape regret? If she did, she would pay a price for such purity. Regrets are more than a difficult feeling. Regrets are clues, signals. If we attend to our regrets— which does not mean harping on them—we learn what we need to do to grow. Knowing what's missing, we can set about supplying the lack, or locating a smart substitute. As she herself had just said, living means making choices, and even right choices entail the loss of possibilities. To regret nothing would be to cease to imagine how things might have been. That would be slow death by spiritual complacency. Sure death for a fiction writer.

No, I don't think my young writer friend will escape regret. She's too curious about the world not to make mistakes, too full of life not to be visited, someday, by at least a few interesting regrets. I think that some day not too far off she will look back on her life with the dismay and wry pity that must attend any close examination of a human being, including oneself, and which result in an expanded sympathy for all human beings. I think she's too intelligent not to discover that regret, too, has been invited to the party and deserves to be—not indulged; shall we say, treated with a certain polite respect?

SELF AND SENSIBILITY: ELIZABETH HARDWICK

A character in Elizabeth Hardwick's second novel, *The Simple Truth*, likes to remind himself that he is more like most of us than he might have been:

> He hated sloth and triviality and would have perished as a pioneer rather than live by his wits as a handsome beau in New York. "This is strangely to my credit," he would think, "since I am a Virginian."

Hardwick, born in Kentucky in 1916, is not like most other southern writers (though her sly wit strikes me as very southern, and the dignity of her intelligence allies her with other serious southern women prose writers, including Eudora Welty, Elizabeth Spencer, and Flannery O'Connor, to name only three who belong to an admirable and continuing tradition). Her novels, condensed to dramatic moment or dialogue, expand philosophically upon reflection. Her essays and criticism, authoritative without being overbearing, proceed by observations and connections and can seem confounding but, in the event, are never willful or irrelevant. She is a careful stylist whose techniques of compression (collage, flashback, ellipsis) strengthen the sense, for the reader, that beneath the considered words beats a powerful heart, that a brave, passionate, and steadfast sensibility, one that may be wounded but wants not to wound in turn, informs the intelligence with a clear awareness of reality. She has created a corpus, amplified by edited volumes of William James's letters, American essays, and fiction by American women, that reaches across half a century to give us a view of literature in our time. Her latest book is a fourth collection of her own essays titled *Sight-Readings* (Random House, 1998), in which, by the way, she notes in an essay on Katherine Anne Porter that "to be a Southern writer is a decision, not a fate."

Hardwick herself left Kentucky for New York City. Marian, the young protagonist of her first novel, *The Ghostly Lover*, makes a similar journey. "It seemed to me a happy circumstance that America should have created a great world city, an intrusive settlement much like a foreign country.... [I]t was the new world for many of us as well as for those from the old world" [from the Afterword].

Again with that sly wit, Hardwick says that "I have never known a family to be entirely pleased by the first printed works of a child. [E]xperience, imagined or otherwise, infects the familiar atmosphere most uncomfortably" [Afterword, *The Ghostly Lover*].

In *The Ghostly Lover*, scenes are constructed of pointillistic sentences that threaten to fly away from one another, leaving our emotions in a void:

> The sun was as clear and white as ice now, and the faint perfume of lilacs blew steadily through the air. In the distance the church bells rang out the time. The illuminated quiet of early afternoon lay over the street. Sometimes the steamy sound of a truck moving over the smooth road could be heard. A bird suddenly stepped in the shadows of the trees.

Menace fills the air but it is a free-floating menace, something on the order of free-floating anxiety but meaner, because it is not subjective but objective: Marian's perceptions approach so close to the edge of an undifferentiated phenomenology that a reader fears to be pushed over, made to realize the lack of support or justification for human feeling and action. And this is just how it is on empty southern streets at noon, with a ruthless sun exposing the harsh truth about our lives....

A bell jar could not better capture the suffocating spirit, the girl caught and conflicted.

It may be that the reader is responding to the "pounding autobiographical stresses in the thoughts of the young girl" [Afterword, *The Ghostly Lover*], who is seeking to understand what it means to be a woman, a woman in the South, a single woman, a married woman.

"I remember telling a young man," Hardwick confesses, "a faithful suitor from 'down home': If my novel is published I will marry you. A wild offer brought on by anxiety. Of course I betrayed him and waved goodbye from the window of the old C&O train that went through the hills of West Virginia, stopped at Washington, and then on to New York" [Afterword, *The Ghostly Lover*].

Publication of *The Ghostly Lover* brought an invitation from Philip Rahv to write for the *Partisan Review*. (*A View of My Own*, published in 1962, is dedicated to Rahv.) She also became a founder of *The New York Review of Books*. Her essays ranged over subjects as disparate as the criminal Caryl Chessman and poet Edna St. Vincent Millay. Of the latter, she points out feelingly, "You cannot give, as she did, your whole life to writing without caring horribly, even to the point of despair" ["Anderson, Millay and Crane in Their Letters," *A View of My Own*]. As for bell jars, writing about Plath she notes, "For all the drama of her biography, there is a peculiar remoteness about [her]" ["Sylvia Plath," *Seduction and Betrayal*]. With the recent appearance of *The Birthday Letters*, the collection of poems by England's Poet Laureate Ted Hughes about his courtship of and marriage to Plath, we may agree even more fervently with Hardwick that "[a] destiny of such violent self-definition does not always bring the real person nearer; it tends, rather, to invite iconography...." ["Sylvia Plath," *Seduction and Betrayal*]. As with pentimento, Hughes's poems add another layer to the portrait, providing us with a new and useful conceptualization at the same time it obscures further the original personality. Hardwick makes the important point that Plath's poems "are about suicide rather than about death" ["Sylvia Plath," *Seduction and Betrayal*] and remarks how eccentric this is, how uncommon in the tradition of English poetry. Writing in the seventies, Hardwick sees Plath as an instinctive feminist, a consciousness-raiser. "I myself do not think her work comes out of the cold war, the extermination camps, or the anxious doldrums of the Eisenhower years. If anything, she seems to have jumped ahead of her dates and to have more in common with the years we have just gone through. . . . What she did not share with the youth of the present is her intense and perfect artistry, her belief in it" ["Sylvia Plath," *Seduction and Betrayal*]. She suggests that a "greed for particulars" characterizes much poetry by women at mid-century, while what is unique about Plath is "the burning singularity of temperament" ["Sylvia Plath," *Seduction and Betrayal*].

Seduction and Betrayal, with its studied attention to writing by women, attracted considerable notice at the time of its publication. Not following any party lines, the book offers superb interpretations of literary works and an opportunity to see how the essayist writes a form of autobiography, allowing us to glimpse the materials and tools she brings to bear. She can be provocative, as when she says of Virginia Woolf that "[her] novels are beautiful; the language is rich and pure, and you are always, with her, aware of genius, of gifts extraordinary and original. Our emotions are moved, at least some of our emotions are moved, often powerfully. And yet in a sense her novels aren't interesting" ["Bloomsbury and Virginia Woolf," *Seduction and Betrayal*]. She can be brusque, as when she precisely isolates the reader's reaction to Theodore Dreiser's *An American Tragedy*:

We know that we are near our own time when a novel can concern itself...with two people, Clyde and Roberta, both deprived, stunted, pitiable. In spite of the equity of deprivation, it is Clyde's lack of resignation to a future darkened by Roberta's pregnancy that moves us, keeps our sense of the intolerable blackness of consequence alive. The mind protests for both of them. It is only that Roberta, trapped, miserable, imagines existence would be possible if only Clyde would take care of her, settle in for life. We cannot quite forgive her the simplicity ["Seduction and Betrayal," *Seduction and Betrayal*].

She can be challenging, as when she declares, "Pride is the way of the tragic Greek heroines—not the answer in the more practical, reduced world of the novel. Here the women must deal with betrayal as a fact of life" ["Seduction and Betrayal," *Seduction and Betrayal*]. Is that true? I am not persuaded that pride motivates all of the tragic Greek heroines, but betrayal is certainly a major theme in the lives of the women who occupy novels. It may be a theme of *Sleepless Nights*, the daring and inventive novel Hardwick published in 1979.

Her provocativeness (sometimes mischievous, sometimes raw), her brusqueness, her unconditional statements requiring the deliberate reader to test insight and observation by specific reference delineate a skeptical, searching mind more intrigued by the truth, or the idea of truth, than by critical or even literary oneups(wo)manship. Because her prose never shows off, because she struggles to stay with thought rather than filigree her sentences with needless allusion, we are fascinated and want to know where this honesty will take us, what conclusions we might ourselves come to if only we pursued our notions more thoroughly, more openly.

A mind so vigorous and equally so vulnerable (as it must be to be open to change and correction) as Hardwick's has power to captivate. Feeling both engaged and protective, the reader must fall a little in love with the writer.

At any rate, that is my experience. In 1983, reviewing Hardwick's *Bartleby in Manhattan*, the third of her collections, in *The New York Times*, Denis Donoghue complained, "She can be laconic, but her ordinary style is lyric or meditative; she likes opulent effects and a well-turned syntax . . . Some of Miss Hardwick's sentences risk the note of incantation." He also objected to the absence of a theoretical apparatus. Sarcastically he says,

> She reads a novel as if it were real life, or an extension of several lives, with the advantage over real life that the novel will wait till she concentrates her mind upon it. I have to report that in her new book she quotes a passage from Kierkegaard which, she may feel, declares criticism in any case an open city. Esthetics, Kierkegaard said, "is a courteous and sentimental science, which knows of more expedients than a pawnbroker." If theories were regarded as expedients in this accommodating spirit, a critic would feel free to get along with nearly any set of them, and would judge the set only upon its practical results; as Elizabeth Hardwick does.

But these criticisms miss the mark. First of all, nobody has accused Elizabeth Hardwick (or anybody else) of stylistic perfection. Second, the attraction of the essay form, even the literary-theory essay, lies in its being a window to the process of thinking. Where prose strives to attract by premises, it is closer to propaganda or rhetoric than to essay.

In her foreword to *Best American Essays 1986*, which she edited, she explains (perhaps with Donoghue in mind?),

> One of the assumptions of the essayist is the right to make his own mistakes, since he speaks only for himself, allowing for the philosopher's cunning observation that "in my opinion" actually asserts "all reasonable men will agree.". . . Expertise, an acquisition promoted by

usefulness, is less cogent to the essay than passion, less to the point than is the soloist's personal signature flowing through the text. Such is the art of the essay.

In other words, self and sensibility are central to Hardwick's understanding of what the essayist does. Hardwick is simply not concerned with what would concern Donoghue. There is really nothing more to be said about this other than, as happens, reviewer and author were poorly matched. In the end, an essay works upon its reader to the extent it holds the reader's interest.

For readers other than Donoghue, *Bartleby in Manhattan*, an admittedly looser compilation of prose pieces, some rather casually occasional, may deepen their affection for the author— the more so as time passes. Collected in 1983, these various compositions, a number of which are about political events and the echoes they raise in contemporary literature, have actually become fresher with time, exact descriptions rescuing the recent past from the welter of reportage and commentary and revivifying history. Lee Harvey Oswald, John Reed and Louise Bryant, Thomas Mann are among the varied subjects. In a discussion of Martin Luther King we encounter Memphis the weekend before the funeral; the city is under curfew:

> The streets are completely empty of traffic and persons and yet the emptiness is the signal of dire and dramatic possibilities. In the silence, the horn of a tug gliding up the dark Mississippi is background. The hotel, downtown, overlooking the city park, is a tomb and perhaps that is usual since it is downtown where nobody wants to go in middle-sized cities.

That is a direct and commanding description, deploying us like troops to 1968. (Note: "The aggressiveness of the essay is the assumption of the authority to speak in one's own voice. . . ." [*Best American Essays*]). Whether history is accidental or fated, it is always attended by melancholy—is it not?—because it is *over*. This note Hardwick sounds stilly in the dark night when she writes, at the end of "The Oswald Family":

> The Warren Report tells a sordid story of greeds too fierce to measure. The greatly favored and the greatly crippled suffer out their destinies. You feel they have been together on the stage for a long time. It was only that the light had not shone in the dingy corners before. There these impatient people, longing for immortality, were waiting to tell us something.

Another of the essays in *Bartleby in Manhattan*, "The Sense of the Present," flings into the general discussion of the contemporary novel several intriguing and implicative comments that obviously have something to say, if only by not saying it, about Hardwick's novels. "Perhaps," she muses, "we cannot demand a 'novel.' " We can say only that a work like *Speedboat* by Renata Adler (a fine novel often spoken of in conjunction with *Sleepless Nights*) is "a novel of some kind." In *Speedboat*, Hardwick tells us, "Space is biography and conflict finally, and going from one place to another is the thread of experience. . . . Perception, then, does the work of feeling and is also the main action. It stands there alone, displacing even temperament."

In *The Simple Truth*, Hardwick had set at stage center a court trial. A young man of uncertain character and ambiguous background, a popular and successful college student, is charged with first-degree murder in the strangulation death of Betty Jane Henderson, the beautiful coed who had "come back for a nightcap" after the dance and whose body, when police arrived, lay on the bed, while "[b]eside her. . . , touching her arm, lay her fur coat."

Yet the novel directs the reader's attention not to this event but to the meanings it assumes for characters who are merely onlookers and not players in the drama. It is as if we are an audience that goes to the theater to watch another audience watching the play. What we see of the play is pretty much incidental; but how it is viewed by the people in the other audience, how they interpret the action and what effect it has on them and how they respond to that effect—all this we see clearly, close up, and are encouraged to reflect upon.

The two characters who are most responsible for mediating the action to us are Joseph Parks, "a large young man of twenty-eight whose spirit was [a?] lively battlefield where fat and nerve contended endlessly," and Anita Mitchell, "an odd-looking woman in a red velvet beret, standing next to him and also alone,... searching her pocketbook for matches." Joseph, an East Coaster newly transplanted to Iowa, intends to be a writer. He loves people en masse and the places where they congregate, and "[t]o hear strains of music as he passed a house or a bar filled him with the joy of life. Sensations of this nature, his pounding heart as he eavesdropped on other people's conversation, had given him the idea that he should be a writer." Anita "was compelled to think about the case, to attend the trial, as a sort of private investigation into the rushing, torrential waters of the unconscious." Where Joseph is content to feel a sympathy for people, Anita wants to know what it means to be a self, a person, a character, what people "mean by *character*." It is Anita who cries out, "They trip you up on an adjective, these lawyers. . . .[Y]ou'd need to think what they would make of it, how the truth, even innocent truth, would be interpreted!" We also meet their spouses and a few acquaintances, and overhear, sometimes, especially at the book's very end, with heart pounding like Joseph's, a great deal of dialogue.

In *Sleepless Nights*, the technique of focusing on the marginal is pushed even farther, for at the center, at the heart of the novel, is only absence. How can we discern margins where the story itself remains unwritten? A woman named Elizabeth writes letters, or rereads letters she has written over a period of years, some of them to a close friend whose initial, *M.*, may stand for Mary McCarthy. Elizabeth has traveled broadly and lived in several places, including Kentucky, New York, Maine, and Boston. In Boston she lived on Marlborough Street. "At last the trees are green on Marlborough Street," wrote Robert Lowell, to whom

Hardwick was married for twenty-three years, in his poem "Man and Wife":

> . . . Oh my *Petite*,
> clearest of all God's creatures, still all air and nerve:
> you were in your twenties, and I,
> once hand on glass
> and heart in mouth,
> outdrank the Rahvs in the heat
> of Greenwich Village, fainting at your feet—
> too boiled and shy
> and poker-faced to make a pass,
> while the shrill verve
> of your invective scorched the traditional South.

Early in the novel, Elizabeth refers to a time when "I was then a 'we.' " She remembers her husband "teasing, smiling, drinking gin after a long day's work" and holding forth on the topic of power and submission in marriage. "Can it be that I am the subject?" she asks herself. The question resonates, referring both to the husband's discourse and her own discourse, the book we are reading.

The book, with its letters, dreams, memories, observations, opinions, brief accounts of other lives, its bits, its snippets, and its scraps of conversation, may be seen as Elizabeth's lifesaver or a record of what she does to save her soul: It is how she makes it through the night(s) without "him." It is, or we think it is, "his" absence that drives her narration, her need to fill the hole he has left with something, some kind of communication. That "he" remains unidentified, barely spoken of, magnifies our sense of his absence and the narrator's loss. Reticence makes the narrator's situation eloquent. Returning to "New York once more, to remain forever, resting on its generous accommodation of women," she is both tough and pathetic, and her sadness spills out in a list of what will be available to her in the city: "Long dresses, arrogance, more chances to deceive the deceitful, confidants, conspirators, charge cards." She apologizes for not writing *Moby-Dick*:

"[N]ever mind that it is the truth. It certainly hasn't the drama of: I saw the old, white-bearded frigate master on the dock and signed up for the journey. But after all, 'I' am a woman."

So the book may be read and has been read as autobiography laid over with the lightest gauze of fiction, but to stop here, thinking that the book has now been summed up, is a mistake, and one that can keep us from seeing the rest that is there. We should be put on the alert when the narrator, as her book nears its end, says in a sighing sort of tone, "Sometimes I resent the glossary, the concordance of truth, many have about my real life, have like an extra pair of spectacles. I mean that such fact is to me a hindrance to memory."

It's safe to say that no writer wishes her novels to be thought of as "mere" autobiography; credit is always due to the imagination for conceiving possibilities where history has only its limited knowledge of the actual. (Historians, memoirists, and autobiographers, however, would do well to steer clear of the current inclination to assume that everything is fiction. Nonfiction is not fiction—not if it is nonfiction. Also, fact is but one of the differences between fiction and nonfiction. But all this is a subject for another essay.) Obviously, some novelists do a better job of imagining than others. Hardwick wrote, in her passage about *Speedboat*, that plotless fiction, to work, must be interesting all along the way. Reading plotless fiction, we cannot say to ourselves that we will tolerate dull stretches for the sake of a dramatic payoff that we know will come. The memories of our narrator Elizabeth in *Sleepless Nights* interest us, partly because they tell us about the world as it is for the people she describes, and partly because we are watching these memories give shape to the narrating self.

On the battered calendar of the past, the back-glancing flow of numbers, I had imagined there would be felicitous notations of entrapments and escapes, days in the South with their insinuating feline accent, and nights in the East, showing a restlessness as beguiling as the winds of Aeolus. And myself there, marking the day with an *I*.

In truth, moments, months, even years were magical.
Pages turned, answering prayers, and persons called out,
Are you there? The moon changed the field to the silvery
lavender of daybreak.

≈:≈

At times I am not certain who is imagining the
working people living in their clashing houses, lying in
their landscape, as if beneath a layer of underclothes. Or
those gathering rubbish, dear indeed to them as relics.
Or those threading through love, missing the eye of the
needle.

Words and rhythms, a waterfall of clauses, blue
lights, amber eyes, the sea under a burning lake. Should
I remember the perfection of a pointed chin and the
abundant, prickly halo of amorous, black Levantine
hair? Or my rival, the girl with the pale-green letter
paper?

What is absorbing and winning about Hardwick's *Sleepless
Nights*, beyond the trenchant and individuating details, is the way
she exposes the process itself: the novelist shows us the complex
interplay between autobiography and fiction, the narrator, so
closely resembling the author, organizing memory and dream,
the public and the private, into a coherence that is herself defined.
If she still is "not certain who is imagining," if she frets that a
"note of irony" falsifies a personal history of loss and suffering, if
she feels that what people know about her can obscure what she
knows about herself, the narrator Elizabeth comes to recognize
her knowledge of *others* as a consolation and a prize. It was how
she got through all those sleepless nights—calling on what she
knows of others, "those whom I dare not ring up until morning
and yet must talk to throughout the night." Similarly, "I love to
be known by those I care for." The absence around which the
book revolves, then, is not her ex-husband's: the absence is that

of the narrator's sense of self, and the progress of the book is the establishment or reclamation of that self.

Moreover, the self is found not in isolation but in community, the community of all those she talks to through the night—including the reader. So the community may not be disturbed in the middle of the night; it *is* there to be called on in the mind, is, that is to say, a literary community, sweet with shared memories of imagined worlds, "escape on the wings of adjectives" from her mother's life and the life men thrust upon women whether they need it or not, life like an unnecessary "pair of reading glasses."

Hardwick, on record as not thinking of herself as a southern writer, is perhaps most not like a southern writer, may be almost an opposite of the southern writer, in this extension of the novel beyond story into an examination of how story fortifies and characterizes self. Her affinities as a writer are to Europeans whose work is marked by a consciousness of the authorial self in relation to cultural history. On the basis of her essays, one might deduce Mann, Pasternak, Nabokov, the poets of civilization and its discontents.

Because as a woman and a writer she stands at an illuminating angle in relation to her southern heritage, because her essays are insightful and informative, because her novels are explorations of novel-writing, and most of all, because her prose is a joy to read, Elizabeth Hardwick is a writer whose body of work deserves consideration as a whole and as a lasting contribution to literature.

I am surrounded by scholars, literary scholars. In the room, they come and go, talking of Michel Foucault. Some of this talk is interesting; some of it is even inspiring. I was once inspired to write a poem about deconstructionism; it was a short poem. On another occasion, writing a longer poem, "Questions and Answers," I found myself secretly amused by the edge of anxiety I'd located in the relationship between Jesus and John the Baptist by calling to mind (my mind, not the reader's) Harold Bloom's *Anxiety of Influence*. I'd not found much convincing in that theory so far as writers' connections to their precursors go, but I was aware that I was speaking to it and being stimulated by it in my poem.

> Did *he* glance startled back at the one who had
>   suddenly recognized him
> disbelieving that the reflection could be greater than
>   the thing reflected?
> Did the anxiety in his heart presage an instant when love

would spin away, screwing itself like a tornado
to a vanishing point, leaving only
the vertigo of despair, the giddy view downward to hell,
or was it merely the consequence, the scar, of
    discovering he had been
from the beginning one who would come after, always
    after,
a feeling as when you sat in study hall
and carefully pulled against the closing of your
    notebook's three rings
at the same time you released the spring, but the snap,
when it came, was too loud anyway, and you made a face
as if to disassociate yourself from the event.

Sometimes I have been prompted into literature by critical notions of a less theoretical kind, caveats ostensibly regarding technique that nevertheless imply a theoretical bias. I wrote a story in the third-person omniscient—my protagonist was God—at least partly just to do it (*tour de force* being one way in which one can have fun), and one of my novels, *In the Wink of an Eye*, metamorphoses the first-person omniscient "I" into God's "eye" as the most efficient mode of transition between scenes in different parts of the world (wherever it glances, there we are). Another short story, "Art and Divine Aberration," is a Siamese twin, with two beginnings conjoined at the climax.

But most of the time, what a writer writes is not much affected by literary criticism. Not even when the writer is someone who is interested in what critics have to say. Not even when she is surrounded by scholars.

Yes, the writer may plunder contemporary criticism for metaphor or argument, the same way she plunders astronomy or paleontology, but these are not influences on her work so much as they are instruments of it. They are tools, or whole wonderful storehouses of tools, that she can use at will to accomplish various tasks, but they don't usually determine which tasks she'll undertake. If she has enough tools at hand, they won't even determine *how* she'll accomplish a task; she can decide how, and then reach for the appropriate instrument.

There is, however, a way in which criticism—most of it not very contemporary, most of it left over from the thirties and forties and fifties—does affect today's literature, determines it: I'm referring to the "applied criticism" sometimes exercised by editors.

For if the advocates of recently popular literary theories such as deconstructionism, Marxism, and feminism have little or no real effect on the writing of fiction today (though they may have an effect on the reading of it), what does have an effect on the writing of fiction is the editor. It is the editor's notions about what constitutes good writing that determines what writing is presented to the reading public. Shockingly, this doesn't mean merely that the editor's taste is reflected in his or her choice of material; it means that the material itself is not infrequently altered by the editor.

What you see is what you get, but it is not always what you should have got.

While this may always have been true—I am not a literary scholar and can't say—it is also true that editorial notions about what constitutes good writing change and that today's editors tend to subscribe to vaguely Hemingwayesque maxims or precepts about how to write that they absorbed as undergraduate English majors.

I've been writing and publishing for a number of years now, and the fact that texts *are* sometimes editorially altered was unknown to me until I began, not long ago, to concentrate on short fiction. (Earlier, there was a little magazine that so changed a story of mine that I was ashamed for people to read it and refused to submit copies to an anthology, but I assumed some extraordinary mistake had been made; it never occurred to me that the changes could have been *purposeful*.) Until then, I had assumed that what I read was what the writer had written. Quizzing my colleagues, I have found that they share this assumption.

I think it might be useful, therefore, to readers of contemporary fiction—to, indeed, the literary scholars I am surrounded by—if I were to present a few examples from my own experience of the ways in which a text may be altered, of how editorial preconceptions about what makes a work of fiction good shape what the critic and scholar read. It may be helpful for them to realize how extensively the text they are deconstructing or psychoanalyzing or politicizing may already have been subjected to a kind of applied criticism. I want to alert critics to the problem of textual authenticity in contemporary publishing.

The first principle of this applied criticism, impressed on every writing and literature student in modern America, is "Show, don't tell." The advice to "show, don't tell" is useful, especially in creative writing classes because almost no beginning writers have anything of interest to tell, though they often have a great deal that is of interest to show. Besides, young writers who haven't much of interest to tell can give their work an appearance of sophistication or knowingness by relentlessly leaving out any attempts at telling. (But if they are completely discouraged from facing their own intellectual clumsiness, they will never make the discoveries about self and world out of which great work grows. They will never deepen a poem's or story's understanding of self and world. So a writing teacher must deliver this advice but not too sweepingly, remembering that it is advice and not a true maxim. It is a really only a sort of mini-maxim.)

Great writing almost invariably "tells," and when editors blue-pencil authorial statement, they deprive the text of its best shot at originality. Imagine Tolstoy's *Anna Karenina* without its opening line: "Happy families are all alike; every unhappy family is unhappy in its own way."

By now, the idea that showing must take precedence over telling is reflexively subscribed to by many editors, who will quickly excise any sentence that threatens to lead the reader away from detail into the thorny thickets of analysis and thought. In this way,

Night is a mystery, a time when we regress to our earlier selves, when we stayed awake listening to our parents rehearse: The Razumovskys spilled beauty on our lids like sand, and we were borne into the world of an ambition that reaches beyond the nameable world. This is our hope: to create, to create, to create, to caress the eye and the ear, to love…

became, when the story, "What I Don't Tell People," appeared in *Mademoiselle* (as "Almost the Real Thing"),

Night is a mystery. I remember when I stayed awake listening to my musician parents rehearse their violins. I lay in bed, the top sheet pulled up tight beneath my chin, drifting into dreams. The Beethoven string quartets spilled beauty on my lids like sand, and I was borne into the world of an ambition that reaches beyond the nameable world. This is our hope: to create, to create, to create, to love.…

In a story set in Honduras, I wanted to give some sense of the layered quality of life there, a sense of how cultural strata, like geological strata, are stacked one atop another, the shape or scape of the present being informed by the configurations of the past. "I was to learn that this was the way here; so often, interiors were larger and more complex than a visitor could guess from the outside," I wrote. "I sometimes had the feeling that the Honduran people were like that too, with secrets an American could never know. The Mayan mysteries had thrived in this country, which ran a topographical gamut from forested mountains to the blue-green Caribbean." In *Redbook*, where the story was printed as "Voyage of the Heart" (and I no longer even remember my original title), my narrator's musings simply came to a sudden stop after "from the outside," the rest of the paragraph consigned to oblivion. (I suppose the written story might be thought of as a substratum of the published story.)

I want to stress that the two editors with whom I worked on these stories were smart, kind, and eager to help me get a paycheck and a publication credit. Both are sophisticated readers, and one is a highly sophisticated writer. It was their *job* to make the fiction in their magazines conform to their readers' perceived expectations.

It is a belief widespread among editors that today's reading public has suffered an attenuation of its attention span mediated by television, as a result of which a story must be dramatic enough to seize the reader at the beginning and short enough to end before the reader's barely sustained attention lapses. I know that Poe wanted to read a story at a single sitting; I don't know that he considered fifteen minutes a sitting. For myself, I rather like a story that forces me, through the intensity of its feeling or thought, to put it down from time to time, to think about it while I am still reading it.

What is lost in this process of making stories speedier and speedier is music, which cannot exist where everything moves at the same fast tempo. The crescendos and diminuendos of passion, the counterpointing of motives, the harmonies that are implied in a linear form by pacing—these are sacrificed to the great god Narrative. (Narrative is a god who, according to acolytes, will brook no deviation from the straight and narrow path of the storyline; but some of us secretly believe the acolytes have misread their god's nature.)

The principle applied here is "If it doesn't bear directly on the story line, leave it out." So much goes that is interesting, intriguing, complicating! Adjectives and adverbs—out. Information about minor characters—out. Description—out. The dome of the state capitol in "What I Don't Tell People" had been "sweet" in manuscript, but "sweet" as an adjective for "dome" was deemed "eccentric" and struck. Like species hunted to extinction, entire sentences vanish, such as the one that said, "The background for all this is populism, a philosophy that says that for every taxpayer there should be two legislators, preferably in conflict with each other." The "all this" wound up with no background—just as, in another country and another story, the Honduran countryside had disappeared, leaving only the foreground of protagonist and plot.

"I sense hidden hysteria and touch her hand, which she is nervously running over the spines of books as if they were a xylophone, as if they could play a tune" is shortened to "I sense hidden hysteria and touch her hand" ("What I Don't Tell People").

Yet another editorial precept carries with it all the weight of an idea grounded in religion and buttressed by the North American belief in utilitarianism. This one says that metaphor is ornament, not meaning.

There is something almost sinful about metaphor and simile, it seems—and if they aren't really sinful, well, they're definitely wasteful. (Which brings us back to "sinful.")

But for writers (this writer, anyway), metaphor is not the trill that graces the note; it is the very theme.

To return to "What I Don't Tell People," take "I introduce him to a young woman with lovely black brows that fly above her face like black swans above a pale wintry marsh." (This line is both an image that heightens the lyrical mood of the story and a setup for the joke that follows it.) The editor says it is too poetic. She wants it changed, and sometimes the writer has an opportunity to make these changes, so now "I introduce him to a lovely young woman with a winter-paled complexion against which her startlingly black brows look like calligraphy." Not as good—there is no real reason in the story for the reference to calligraphy, the young woman's complexion is prosaically rather than poetically rendered—but less outré, and not bad. When I read the published story, I find that I have introduced the male character to "a lovely young woman coworker," period. There are too many syllables in the noun phrase, "coworker" clunks, and the punch line that follows has lost its punch.

But the story line is unscathed.

"I watched as he set his coffee cup down, carefully guiding it to the saucer's center" was once "I watched as he carefully fitted the bottom of the cup to the plateau at the saucer's center, as if he were guiding it to a landing in a small field" ("Voyage of the Heart").

When the narrator of "What I Don't Tell People" refers to the baby she hopes "is writing itself into existence right now, a character sketch polishing itself in my body," and the character sketch is erased in proofs, the reader may well wonder what kind of pregnancy is going on here, not understanding that a metaphor has been aborted.

That reader, or the editor's idea of the reader, must never be offended. (One caveat that is not derived from Hemingway.) "His shirt rode up, exposing a tummy that was practically asking to be patted," is okay if you don't add "like a tortilla." Elsewhere, "[H]e swallowed a host of sleeping pills, dozens of them, red and white and yellow like the races of the world" must be changed to "like some of the races of the world" in order not to omit anyone unfairly.

This reader is not really very bright. He or she may be discomposed by the phrase "how love anchors us," thinking that the writer has said that only love can anchor us, and will rest easy only if the phrase is changed to "how love helps to anchor us." Similarly, "the jeep of many colors" finds itself removed from the story—towed off to the parking lot of the margin—because the reader will not, the editor is certain, recognize the allusion.

Editors sometimes worry that, although they themselves recognize the complexities of the classics, today's readers cannot grasp a work of fiction unless it has a message, a clearly stated thesis.

What a blow to Keats's idea of negative capability!—but negative capability has been in disfavor with our publishing industry ever since sales figures, which respond more quickly to sentimentality than to ambiguity, became the deciding factor in decisions to publish (it was not always thus).

Let me shift from short stories to novels for a minute. I have to state that the whole idea of a novel's possessing a thesis runs counter to my approach to writing one, and indeed, I would never have written one if I thought that in doing so I was presenting a single thesis. I always start with a question, one which, it seems to me, can be—has to be—answered both "yes" and "no" with equal validity and force of feeling. Am I my sister's keeper, even if that entails martyrdom? Yes. And no. The novel, *Sick and Full of Burning*, provides both answers, supplying equally weighted evidence (the character says "no" but acts out "yes").

I imagine deconstructionists may be pleased to come across such contradictions, but truth to tell, they probably are not half so pleased as the writer, since such a contradiction is usually precisely the point at which she was able to say, Aha, I have an idea for a novel. Feminists and Marxists, and Freudians, of course, insist on theses.

So do some editors, who will not publish a story unless the ending is rewritten "to bring the message into focus."

And if there is no message? If the *message* of the story is *that* there is no message? If the writer works to place the reader in a position that will compel him toward his own conclusions?

To bring the reader to a full sense of his own freedom—now *that's* a message.

A corollary to the preceding says that characters must act in accordance with one or two unconflicting psychological principles.

Here we have the commonly accepted idea that characters must be predictable, though of course preferably not predicted; that is, the writer is called on to give her readers personae whose actions, when we think about them, could be deduced in advance from their characters, though to avoid boredom, these characters should be presented to us in such a way as to outpace our deductions by a logical step or two.

One "advantage" of this predictability is that the characters who exhibit it can serve as role models or cautionary examples for the reader, who is assumed to need guidance in how to live, assumed also to be reading in search of that guidance.

(Perhaps the Freudian belief in psychological consistency is not far removed from the Victorian hope of self-improvement.)

I tell my students that if they want to get published they should follow this rule. If they want to create characters who will live, they will embed in the heart of each a contradiction. Contradiction creates energy; the struggle toward resolution impels character toward plot. This is why Augusta, in *Augusta Played*, is willing to be, when the situation (a comic one) calls for it, a topless flutist: she is so serious about her work that she will do whatever is necessary to call attention to it; she is so determined to be loved (by the world) that she will sacrifice love (her husband's). This is why her husband, Norman, cleaves to a deterministic view of psychology, while so terrified of the possibility of arbitrary hurt that he tries to make Augusta conform to what he knows, instead of allowing himself to learn from her. This is why, in another novel, revolutionaries like Rosita reveal themselves as conservatives and conservatives like the Queen Mother disclose that they are, at heart, revolutionaries: in their case, which is *In the Wink of an Eye*, their contradictions move them not only into the book's plot but out of it, via spaceship.

I am sure that other writers could draw additional assumptions out of their experiences with editorial alteration. These seem to me to be the main ones I have garnered.

Maybe, as I say, editors have always felt they could alter texts without the writer's consent. (They sometimes seem to think they can do it even without the writer's knowledge. I remember that when I was working as an assistant in a children's book publishing office the art department and my boss both assured me it was "all right" for them to delete or change words in order to make the text "fit" on the page. The author, they said, would never notice the changes. I can only say that when I complete a manuscript, of whatever length, I have arrived at a considered decision about every comma in it, and while editorial suggestions and corrections of typos are very welcome, an editorial presumption that I don't know or care what I've written is not.) Maybe editors have always felt they could tell an author to "add word to fill," meaning a simple "potion" must become a "powerful potion" in order to prevent the eyesore of a "widow," a line with too few characters. Maybe editors have always revised punctuation and paragraphing without informing the author.

Maybe magazines have always felt they could chop a story to make room for ad copy.

But whether or not that is so, or to whatever extent, there are things about this situation that make it particularly important as it exists *now*. For one thing, for many writers, because of the drastically increasing reluctance of trade houses to publish serious literature, magazine publication may be their texts' only appearance in print. They can no longer count on subsequent book publication as an opportunity to "get it right." The critic who (the writer hopes) one day inspects magazine publications must bear in mind that he or she may be treating a corrupted text. The apparently original text may be a later version, devised for or even by the magazine.

For another thing, in the age of word processors, some authors' preferred texts may be all the more difficult to recover, since the latest entry on disk file will appear to be the corrected one unless the author has gone to the trouble of noting that it was for magazine publication only. Not only may the magazine version as it appeared be a deviant from the original, but the most recent version on the disk may only represent an attempt to arrive at the magazine version, which was finally done by the editor.

Why do writers go on publishing in magazines that trespass on their work? I know why I do, why I even embrace every chance to, though I also dream of the day when, like Hemingway, I can demand a clause in my contract that legislates against an editor's changing so much as a comma without my say-so: for the credit, which may someday persuade a publisher of my potential for commercial "viability."

And we oughtn't forget that magazines, even the slick ones most given to a presumption of editorial authority, are at least open to new work in a way that trade book publishers today are, alas, not. The magazine does not need to sell itself on the basis of its story writer's name, though it may choose to do so; it *can* include a story by an unknown, or a relative unknown, or it can include the known writer's less commercial work. Writers agree (tacitly) to this situation because it is a way to find readers, and writers want readers. They are grateful to editors who help them find them.

(But some magazines' publishers require them to conduct polls to determine how many readers various elements of the issue have attracted. You may think of it as a kind of Nielsen's ratings system for print media.)

And the wise writer knows that some of those editorial changes will be good ones, worth incorporating in the final manuscript if it *does*—O happy day—find book publication.

Still, something sad is going on here, something rather decadent and pitiable: America is losing its voice. What kind of cultural discourse can there be when book publishers no longer dare to publish the new, the eccentric, or the unpopular, and when magazine editors put their own words into their authors' mouths, or take authors' words out? When the authentic text remains outside the published text, in the margin, the author has been similarly removed, shunted to the sidelines of intellectual society. There exist the little magazines, of course, where much of the best work of today *is* to be found (despite Richard Ford's doubts, expressed in *Harper's*), but it is difficult to conduct a serious forum with a handful of participants.

If I could make a wish for my country, it would be—along with the usual and essential Utopian wishes for an end to poverty, to drugs, to racism—that we could *in fact* claim for ourselves the freedom of thought and expression that we have declared ourselves entitled to but seldom exercise. We would be a country that dares to speak for itself, that dares to let its people, including its writers, speak for themselves.

I exaggerate, I know. But to effect, I hope.

Meanwhile, we can at least tip our readers off, let them know that when we, writers, appear to be speaking for ourselves, we are not always doing so. Sometimes editors are speaking for us. Sometimes editors are saying, in so many words, only what some critics or scholars taught them twenty years ago, in Sophomore Lit. (What will we do, then, if, in time, they begin to edit according to the principles of Michel Foucault?)

THE DARESOMENESS OF A SOUTHERN WOMAN WRITER

More and more of us," writes Bobbie Ann Mason in her lovely memoir, *Clear Springs*, "are rummaging in the attic, trying to retrieve our history. . . .We seem to hope that if we can find out our family stories and trace our roots and save the old cookie jars and coal scuttles, we just might rescue ourselves and be made whole."

The genealogical impulse that seizes us in the middle years—Mason's generation is slightly pre-boomer, the later years of the so-called Silent Generation—is not necessarily the same impulse that has produced the recent memoir craze. Or let's acknowledge that there are different kinds of memoirs, and Mason's, with its attention directed outward toward forebears and the legacies of other lives, its gentle poking into formerly closed closets and filial salvaging of memories, offers us something closer to a personal history, a multigenerational narrative tracing a lineage of love and loss in rural America.

It is, of course, "the old cookie jars and coal scuttles" that seize *us*, that lend warmth, reality, and excitement to memory.

Raised on a farm in the Jackson Purchase in western Kentucky,
Mason knew a hardscrabble childhood of crops, cows, chickens,
and church, which she describes exactly, in a landscape that she
limns with the delicatest detailing:

> Earnest Mrs. Roberts in her Easter hat pumped the
> pedals of the piano along with "Up from the Grave He
> Arose" until we thought we would rise up on Easter,
> too.... I loved the round silver tray of minuscule tinkling
> glasses nesting in their little holes like the marbles in
> Chinese checkers. . . .
>   Daddy simply stayed home. He would have none
> of it.

She describes a christening as "baby-sprinkling": "a wet rose
shaken on a baby's head." And who would not be charmed by
her account of the first-grade pageant:

> Miss Christella assigned me to be a daffodil in a
> pageant. Mama bought the yellow crepe paper to make
> the daffodil dress.
>   "This won't do," she said doubtfully when she spread
> the length of crinkly crepe paper next to me. "Yellow's
> not your color."
>   Mama drove to school and informed Miss Christella
> that yellow was not my color. Blue was my color, because
> of my eyes. Yellow made me look sickly. "She has to be
> a bluebell," Mama said firmly. "Bobbie's not a March
> flower."
>   Mama exchanged the yellow crepe paper for blue
> and I became a bluebell.

I met Bobbie Ann Mason a few months ago; she is quiet, in a
way that suggests both a habit of removal and an observant cast of
mind. Perhaps she's a bit shy, though, as her story makes apparent,
she has always been assertively curious. Her parents, without
benefit of much formal education for themselves, seem to have

been amazingly supportive, encouraging her whole-heartedly in
her academic and literary ambitions, in almost everything, in fact,
including her teenage enthusiasm for the Hilltoppers, a singing
quartet of students from Western Kentucky State College. "The
Hilltoppers' style wasn't exactly Big Bill Broonzy and it wasn't
rock-and-roll yet either . . . but it grabbed me and shook me up
like a religious vision, a calling." A girl who could start a fan club
and write and distribute a newsletter would be bound to head
off to college and later ride a bus to New York City. Next came
graduate school, marriage, and critical and commercial success
as a writer, beginning with her first book of fiction, *Shiloh and
Other Stories.* It is clear, when she says of her mother that "[s]he
had resilience, verve, and what she called daresomeness," that
Bobbie Ann is her mother's daughter.

As daughters' books do, hers tends to focus on her mother
and grandmother (but the men are by no means neglected). It
would be hard, in any case, not to be magnetized by a mother
whose homemaking required her to be "always butchering and
plucking and planting and hoeing and shredding and slicing and
creaming (scraping cobs for the creamed corn) and pressure-
cooking and canning and freezing and thawing and mixing and
shaping and baking and frying." One can taste the down-home
meals that resulted.

In graduate school in Binghamton, New York, Mason
"yearned for the long, languorous springtime of Kentucky. I
craved the mellow air that seemed to caress every pore. I wanted
tulips and redbud and dogwood blossoms." She would discover
that "I could draw on my true sources in order to write fiction.
How could I have failed to recognize them? They had claimed
me all along. So much of the culture that I had thought made me
inferior turned out to be my wellspring. And my mother was my
chief inspiration."

Now, she writes, she lives near where she grew up, "on my own
piece of ground with my husband and pets," but it's a different
life. "In sophisticated gatherings," she notes mischievously, "I'm
sometimes given to conversation stoppers. I might mention the
time I sang with a gospel quartet, or how my family didn't have

an indoor bathroom until I was eight years old, or how I had to sleep with a pan to catch the water from the leak in the ceiling. I might let slip that my Granny made her hair curlers out of pipe cleaners with scraps of leather." There's that "daresomeness" again. And yet again, in a powerful scene of her mother, seventy-seven, arthritic, with osteoporosis and having survived a stroke, as she takes off to the farm pond by herself to go fishing:

> She had never felt such a huge fish pulling at her. With growing anticipation, she worked the fish for an hour or more. But time seemed to drift like a cloud... She thought she knew exactly which fish she had hooked. She had had her eye on it for years. It was the prize fish of the whole pond. She had seen this great fish now and then, a monster that would occasionally surface and roll. It would wallow around like a whale. Since the first time she'd seen it, she had been out to get the "old big one." Her quest had become legendary in the family.

Legendary in literature, too, as this is surely a version of Ahab and his whale, of *The Old Man and the Sea*, an inland voyage to the depths of the unknown. "I read so much into my parents," she admits. "I read the character and history of America in them as if they were a book." She has written that book, and it is full of feeling for language and literature, her family and home, and our country and history.

THE GLOBE AND THE BRAIN:
ON PLACE IN FICTION

Fiction is about people making something happen or responding to something happening. Everything that happens happens somewhere. It takes place. Therefore fiction, also, takes place.

Of course, the place may be an imaginary place. It may be a room in an unidentified city. It may be indoors or outdoors. It may be someone's mind. Writers will go anywhere, and why not?

But most of the time writers stick close to home: William Faulkner's "postage stamp" of Yoknapatawpha, Eudora Welty and her brilliantly vivid Mississippi Delta, Flannery O'Connor and Georgia, Mary Ward Brown and Alabama, Fred Chappell and North Carolina. Or think instead of Saul Bellow and Chicago, Willa Cather and the Plains, Wallace Stegner and the West and Midwest. Think of the New Englanders.

Most of these writers set their stories and novels, or in some cases essays, in the place they knew best, usually the place where they grew up. They knew, or know, that place in their bones, which means knowing not only its weathers, landscape, people, language, social culture, emotional climate, flora, and fauna, but even its rhythms. From the fast-talking shtick and caffeinated philosophical riffs of Bellow's savvy but hurting protagonists to Faulkner's stubborn obsessives, rhythm is part of the apparatus for defining place for the reader. Think of Eudora Welty's great short story "Powerhouse," in which the rhythms of black jazz and Delta blues allow us to experience a concert as if we were there. The band "Powerhouse and His Tasmanians" is on tour and playing at a "white dance."

"You need to see him," Welty tells us. "He's going all the time, like skating around the skating rink or rowing a boat. It makes everybody crowd around, here in this shadowless steel-trussed hall with the rose-like posters of Nelson Eddy and the testimonial for the mind-reading horse in handwriting magnified five hundred times. Then all quietly he lays his finger on a key with the promise and serenity of a sibyl touching the book." Before they tackle a piece Powerhouse makes the band come together in a hush. "His hands over the keys, he says sternly, 'You-all ready? You-all ready to do some serious walking?'—waits—then, STAMP. Quiet. STAMP, for the second time. This is absolute. Then a set of rhythmic kicks against the floor to communicate the tempo. Then, O Lord! say the distended eyes from beyond the boundary of the trumpets. Hello and good-bye, and they are all down the first note like a waterfall."

The story fills up with music. In fact, the story *is* music, the unnamed narrator and Powerhouse and his Tasmanians speaking in idiomatic rhythms that create a musical conversation—or say a musical community in which black and white are equally voiced, equally honored.

It's thought that Welty wrote this story in a single burst after seeing Fats Waller in concert, but she couldn't have done it if she weren't already intimate with the vernacular of the Deep South.

~:~

In her seminal essay "Place in Fiction," Welty calls place "one of the lesser angels," important for clarifying character and making the world the character inhabits one that seems, to the reader, real. She defines "place in fiction" as "the named, identified, concrete, exact and exacting, and therefore credible, gathering spot of all that has been felt, is about to be experienced, in the novel's progress." *Moby-Dick* could not take place in Kansas. Huck Finn would not be Huck Finn without the Mississippi River. The Comptons are who they are because of how they respond to the place in which they find themselves, namely, a segregated South. Ellen Gilchrist's wild and crazy women have to deal with a society that wants them to behave like "ladies." Joyce Carol Oates's characters contend with a bleakness and a coldness that would make their struggle seem almost futile except for the passion they bring to it.

A lesser angel then, but one essential, if fiction is to shine in all its glory.

~:~

As mentioned above, most writers begin with a sense of their own place, their homeplace, where they were introduced to reality, the world around them. Fred Chappell's upbringing in Canton, North Carolina, is reflected in both his stories and his poetry and is *inflected* by a gentle magical realism that carries his world into a realm of timelessness. Lee Smith's hilarious stories about Appalachian women have the wiry toughness of bluegrass music and truck farmers. But not all of us are that closely linked to our origins.

I was born in Louisiana, spent my childhood in Ithaca, New York, and grew up outside Richmond, Virginia, in places very different from one another and now so different from what they were when I was there that they no longer seem like home. I have few memories of Louisiana, and most of them are mixed up with memories of what my parents told me about it. Ithaca, when we lived there, was a postwar town struggling out of the Great Depression: we lived in a tenement building above a grocery store; it's now Yuppified, gentrified, and a great place to shop for clothes.

My college years included a semester each in Socorro, New Mexico, and Knoxville. In my adulthood I have lived in North Carolina; New York City; southwest Minnesota; England; Madison, Wisconsin; Bellingham, Washington; Memphis; Huntsville, Alabama; and a part of Virginia called Southside, where my husband and I live now. I've traveled to Europe, Latvia, Russia (then the Soviet Union), Helsinki, Canada, the Yucatán, and the Philippines. I feel closest to the South, but I do not feel particularly Virginian, or that Virginians have any particular interest in my work. Madison, Wisconsin, where I taught at the university, is still close to me, although I always thought it was a really weird place, with lovely, goodhearted people and bizarre politics. I loved my time in Huntsville, and would love to be an Alabaman—except that I'd deeply miss the look and smell of Virginia.

This confusion—or perhaps it would be more accurate to say *diffusion*—of identity is not peculiar to me. I know people who have moved more than I have and many people who have traveled more. In his recent collection of essays, *Where the Southern Cross the Yellow Dog*, critic and scholar Louis D. Rubin, Jr., refers to fictional characters who "grow out of an emotional relationship to the place and are manifestations of the imaginative experience of the locales in their creators' own lives."

Where can any of us find the fictional characters who "are manifestations of the imaginative experience of the locales in" our own lives?

My first two novels were set in New York City. I'd lived there for five years as a young wife and feminist divorcée. The first, *Sick and Full of Burning*, was about a young woman who, post-marriage, goes to medical school and consciousness-raising sessions. The second, *Augusta Played*, was about a mixed marriage in the sixties and the complications that families can create for a young couple. In both books, the female protagonist was a displaced southerner trying to adjust to the big city. As relative newcomers, they had a reason to pay close attention to the places where they were living now. In *Sick and Full of Burning*, Tennessee Settleworth is paying for med school by working as a live-in tutor, a latter-day governess. When Tennessee applies for the job, the girl she is to tutor meets her at the door.

> ...Cameron led the way into her room, explaining what would be expected of me. I was to tutor her in all of her subjects. "I don't know geography," I panicked; "I don't *know* French."
> "That's all right," she said. "I don't either."
> [T]he two of us found Mrs. Carlisle in her bedroom, munching Hershey bars. She had on a pink quilted robe that went nicely with her cropped red hair. "How do you do," she said, turning off the television set by remote control. "Cameron's grades are terrible."
> "You know that it will be ten dollars an hour . . . ."
> "I don't see why not," she sighed. "It's only a fraction of what the Black Panthers take."

But my third novel takes place in a country I have never been to: Bolivia. I tried to go there, but shortly before I was to leave, they had another of their many coups, and the State Department advised U.S. citizens to stay away. I wound up going to the Yucatán instead—which, actually, did give me a sense of climate, landscape, visual culture. I located a botanist at the University—I was in Madison by now—and quizzed him at considerable length and on numerous occasions, even checking some of the manuscript with him. For the rest, I read books.

Why was I even trying to write about a place that, for me, was about as familiar as ancient Mesopotamia? I had to. I had a story and a point to make, both about revolution. *In the Wink of an Eye* could take place only in a landlocked country. In Africa that would have been Uganda, where Idi Amin was wreaking horror and horrible suffering. I wanted to write a comedy, not a tragedy. I'm not sure my novel could be set in Bolivia today, but at the time, the place was remote enough from everyday life in the U.S. that it could sustain an aura of fantasy. The sky in Bolivia could be filled with brightly colored birds. The mountains could be topped with snow. The jungle could be both flowerful and mysterious. Write about what you know, we are often advised, but Welty says, "It is both natural and sensible that the place where we have our roots should become the setting, the first and primary proving ground, of our fiction. Location, however, is not simply to be used by the writer—it is to be discovered, as each novel itself, in the act of writing, is discovery."

I had a marvelous time in Bolivia even though I wasn't there physically. There were six main characters, plus the Pope and the Queen Mother and a kitten named Nameless. As those who were guerilla fighters traveled through the Green Hell, they tended to chores besides guerilla fighting, such as "bandaging bleeding feet and stewing cat meat" (but not Nameless!), "scrubbing rags of clothes on stones with green berries for soap, pulling a grateful passing peasant's rotten teeth."

The leader, Miguel, and his second-in-command, Ramón, oversee the development of the Green Hell, an essential step in their campaign to return Bolivia to the Bolivians:

> The sleepy rivers of the jungle were being awakened by new travelers upon them, virginal rivers penetrated by the insolent lanchas bearing equipment. Reedy passageways parted. Trees over a hundred and eighty feet high, some already dead, were felled, an immense task because their apparently endless trunks were trapped in an elaborate network of smaller trees, woody lianas, and creeper vines. Some of the trees had enormous flat plank roots. Miguel's men swung their machetes. The tall, fallen, defeated trees, bleached by moonlight, were like the carcasses of sharks fouled in safety nets. When they dried up, the men burned or bulldozed them. Drilling equipment, dragged for miles through the jungle and relayed across rivers by pulleys, lay under tarpaulin in the same soft, muted moonlight. In the camp, radios played dance music, as faint as if it were an echo of itself. People played poker. Ping-Pong. Rolled dice. And at

the camp's edge, behind mammoth trees and thick grass, men and women made love.

Butterflies, folding their forewings over their backs, gathered in sleeping assemblies for the night, hundreds to a branch—the same branch they returned to each migration. A howler monkey screamed. A timamo ruffled her wings, floated an inch off her perch, settled down again, and tucked her head beneath her wing. A snake slid silkily as a live scarf down a wire-thin smooth-barked liana, as if wrapping itself around a woman's neck—quick and deadly embrace. A heavy silence dropped over the jungle, a shroud. Night died into midnight.

Rosita, in her little tin-roofed shack, slept in Miguel's arms, but her dreams were uneasy, unfulfilled. The sad-faced kitten curled between them, its fur as soft as a sigh against Rosita's sleeping wrist.

Whether you know a place or not, detail is what convinces the reader that you do. Fiction, after all, is a lie. It needs to be a *convincing* lie. Science fiction and fantasy provide details to draw us into the story. At the same time, Harry Potter comes alive because he grows and changes like boys who are not wizards. Fantastical beings have a way of being very like humans. If they weren't, we wouldn't be interested in reading about them. If you write a story about stones, the stones will take on human characteristics, or the reader will stop reading.

Many writers have had the odd experience of finding their work read as if it were autobiographical when it isn't and as if it were not when it is. What makes the difference is not what did or didn't happen to the writer but how well—or not—she created it. To repeat Welty, a well-described place goes a long way toward making the story credible.

༺∴༻

I was offered a job in Arizona that I turned down because I was afraid I might never be able to discover the poems in that beautiful, but to me unknown, landscape. Even in Madison, which has plenty of leafy trees, nine years passed before I began to write fiction that was set there. It took me that long to learn Wisconsin's paradoxes. These paradoxes were rendered nearly invisible (to me, at least) by the overlay of populism and a steady midwestern optimism.

In the South, paradox comes right up to you and bites you. Elegant gardens, and Elvis on velvet. Fainting belles with backbones of steel. Good ol' boys who know Latin. Fundamentalists, and book lovers who cherish southern literature. It's black and white. The Midwest is gray—until you've been there long enough for your eyes to adjust to the subtle gradations of hue. In a dialogue included in my collection *Writing the World*, poet and southerner Henry Taylor mentions his Quaker background and points out that "there are contradictions and tensions between those two cultural inheritances," which he has found useful in his writing. But, as someone else once said to me, in Madison it's hard to tell the Congregationalists from the Unitarians.

Nevertheless I had begun to notice things, like the law that said blind people were not allowed to hunt unless accompanied by a sighted person. I noted, and would write in my book *My Life and Dr. Joyce Brothers* a novel in stories, that "[w]e march against U. S. imperialism and big brotherism and send Joe McCarthy to the Senate," that "[w]e tax people out of sight to support social agencies and then pass a Grandparent Liability Act to make private citizens ineligible for state aid." Then there was the time I was reading a poem at an open-air poetry festival downtown and getting more laughs than I'd anticipated: it was a funny poem, but maybe not that funny. As I left the podium to return to my seat facing the street, I realized that I'd been upstaged by the Oscar Meyer weinermobile, whose driver must have been curious about what was going on. I felt I was ready to start writing about Wisconsin—which, by the way, is pronounced by natives as "Wi-scon-sin." The rest of us say "Wis-con-sin." The first story I wrote that was set in Madison was called "War and Peace," and shortly after that I realized that if I added to it about three pages from an old, abandoned manuscript, and stuck in some other bits and pieces I had on hand, I had the scaffolding for a book of stories set in Madison. I already had a title: *My Life and Dr. Joyce Brothers.*

I had noticed that the state mental hospital was across the lake from the University. Trying to register both the light and the dark of that scene I wrote, in one of the stories:

> The lake is blue with flashing white lights. Sailboats tack back and forth against the wind. Students, one of the three principal products of Madison (the other two being doctors and lawyers), stroll by the lakeshore, wearing cut-off jeans, T-shirts, backpacks, and no shoes. Across the lake stands the State Hospital for the Insane.
>
> Ronnie and I find a bench near the lake's edge. We take off our shoes like the students, stretch out our legs and let our toes wave semaphorically to the open air. The reddened sun radiates throbbing waves like a commercial for a painkiller—a sore spot on the sky. A cloud like a Band-Aid comes along and covers it.
>
> In the muted light, the lake no longer looks blue—it's green, with cold, black shadows. Bees are falling out of the sky like an Egyptian plague. They hang in front of our faces as if they've forgotten how to fly, or don't feel like it. Dead fish wash up against the pier. The lake is so full of chemicals, any day it could explode.
>
> I brush the bees away from in front of my face and ask Ronnie if she's decided yet what she's going to do after Paul dies. This is something we've been talking about on and off, ever since they got the news.

Actually, *my* title was "My Life *with* Dr. Joyce Brothers," but the publishing house lawyer worried that a dissatisfied reader might sue the publisher for promising the inside dope on Dr. Joyce Brothers and delivering only some literary fiction that had nothing to do with her. We even sent galleys to her; she had no problem at all with my use of her name.

I used real place names, included landmarks such as the state capitol building—"In the middle of the Square stands the state capitol, a building that is like a *frisson* made visible, a delicate shiver of white stone"—and community events such as the Farmers' Market. I used real street names. A few people were disturbed by this, as if it had never been done before, but I suppose when we read *Ulysses* we tend not to notice, unless we're familiar with Dublin, that James Joyce does it too.

It was a lot of fun to be writing about the city. I felt there were things to be said about the place—comic things, sad things, and lovely, mellow things—and it was a kind of relief to anchor the stories to the city instead of only my own consciousness, or, rather, Nina's consciousness, for she was the narrator and, by the way, yet another transplanted southerner. I also believed that Madison was the right place for a book about life in America at the turn of the twenty-first century, that it was the heart of the heartland.

Nina is dealing with the loss of the family she was born to. She hopes for a child of her own and is willing to undertake the unusual in search of one. A short-short, tucked in right after the stories about her family of origin, before she begins her quest, is titled "The Parents." Here it is, the whole thing:

We bring our babies, blue-eyed babies, brown-eyed babies; we have come to watch the parade, the marching bands. Young women step high; batons fly, flash against the sky like lightning rods. Oh, spare the child, for next come the floats. See Mickey Duck! See Donald Mouse! Snow White rides in her pumpkin carriage, faster, faster, speeding toward marriage with the prince who will give her babies, blue-eyed babies, brown-eyed babies, like our own babies, who are—lost. Lost at the parade! Where are our babies, our babies? We are looking for them everywhere, frantically, everyone helping and shouting: Find the babies!—when suddenly we see them. No wonder no one could find them. They have grown three feet taller, sprouted whiskers or breasts, swapped spun sugar for Sony Walkmen. We kiss them and hug them, but we are secretly frightened by their remarkable new size. They tell us not to worry. They will take care of us. And sure enough, later, we let them drive us home, because their eyes are sharper, their hands are steadier, and they know the way, which we forget more and more often. They stroke our hair and tell us to be calm. On Saturday, our babies help us to choose the best coffin. They are embarrassed when we insist on taking it home to try it out, but they give in because they don't want to upset us. After they leave for the cinema, we climb into the coffin and pull the lid over us. The salesman had said one wouldn't be big enough, then said one would not be sanitary. We laughed. Age has shrunk us. We are small enough to fit in here quite comfortably. It is as dark as a movie house, the kind in which we used to neck in the back row. Now, of course, nothing is playing. The film has completely unwound, and the only sound is the flicking of the loose end, around and around.

There's no autobiography here, and no place besides a parade. But I remembered my mother telling me about the dream she had when she was a young mother with her first child, my brother. She dreamed she was in a telephone booth, and while she was dialing, Mike kept getting bigger and bigger, and the bigger he got, the more scared she was. How could she ever take care of him? How could she ever discipline him? I think that place—that place of anxiety—is one many parents must know. It's an interior place, and I'll talk about interior places in a moment.

Although I thought of *My Life and Dr. Joyce Brothers* as a collection of stories, the publisher brought it out as "a novel in stories," which meant it was marketed and reviewed as a novel. Because the book did have an overarching narrative—how a single woman deals with the loss of one family and acquires another— this didn't bother me, but shortly after the book appeared, while

I was walking my cairn terrier, a line came into my head: "At five-thirty I pick up my wife and she says Let's take home Thai." I have no idea where the line came from; I suspect the "t's" had something to do with why it stayed with me. But who was saying it? Where did his wife work? Why take-out?

I realized then that I was not done with my Madison stories. In *My Life and Dr. Joyce Brothers* Nina Bryant had been surrounded by friends and neighbors who were important to her, and evidently, they wanted their own stories told. It was, as it turned out, Larry Adcock who was picking up his wife, a lawyer, and they took home take-out because their marriage was too shaky for them to spend time cooking together. After the divorce, Larry will briefly date Nina's friend Sarah, an art gallery-owner. Sarah and Nina often go to the Farmers' Market on Saturday mornings, where they run into Ian and Shelley, respectively a high-school French teacher and a nurse, whose daughter, Isabel, is soon to come out to them. Meanwhile, a young black woman has moved into the neighborhood, feeling a little lonesome and out of place:

She didn't even know everybody yet!

She didn't know the couple with the three boys. She'd see them hanging out in the yard in the late afternoon, playing ball or tag, but they seemed so contained, a unit, that she never did more than nod. In the late afternoon they called to one another, the parents to the boys, the boys to their parents, the boys among themselves, and their voices were a suburban choir, a cookout a capella. As the sun dropped lower it seemed to be slipping from a grasp, falling from the sky, as if accidentally let go; it rolled down the long, straight streets to the precipice of horizon and went right over the edge, a kind of Chappaquiddick—the way all can change in a moment, the fatal mistake—and the night, instead of cooling off, grew warmer. It was going to be a steambath summer, neighbors rising at six to mow the lawn before the day was too hot to think of any task more arduous than drinking iced tea. Sun-brewed-and-herbal iced tea, because that was the kind of city this was. This was the kind of city that, when you got off the plane coming back from anywhere, St. Louis or Atlanta or Seattle, and you flagged a cab because the limo was never there, the cab driver had a Kundera novel and a plastic bottle of spring water in the front seat beside him, and when you asked him if he liked the novel he said he wasn't far along enough to compare it with Kundera's previous books. All in all, it was that kind of a city.

I made up a couple of civic events, one being "the Six-State Calliope Conference" and another "the Merchants' Parade." Only after I'd made up the Merchants' Parade did I learn that Madison does indeed have something like that, although I don't remember the name of it. Before the parade begins, Nina and her daughter walk up State Street, taking in the "whiff of dope as we passed Rose Records, the sinuous jangle of Middle Eastern music as we passed Zorba's, the Indian vendor politely peddling pita, the bright colors of sweaters from The Gap, [and] the wind off the lake that smelled of clogged algae." The biker convention and Dairy Month, when cows graze on the grass in Capitol Square and, if you want, you can *milk* one, were real! Madison, the place, had become a community.

In his essay "The Sense of Place," Stegner sums up Kentucky writer Wendell Berry's thinking on the subject: "If you don't know where you are . . .you don't know who you are." Stegner suggests that not only is the self unformed without a place but place itself is not real "until people have been born in it, have grown up in it, lived in it, known it, died in it—have both experienced and shaped it, as individuals, families, neighborhoods, and communities, over more than one generation. Some are born in their place, some find it, some realize after long searching that the place they left is the one they have been searching for. But whatever their relation to it, it is made a place only by slow accrual, like a coral reef."

I decided to underscore this reality by ending the sequel, titled *The Society of Friends*, with the same line with which I opened it, as if to put a fence around the neighborhood.

In the course of writing *The Society of Friends*, I was surprised to realize that not even this second book would encompass the world I was creating, a world that grew out of a real place but now had its own real and unique identity. I now began to grasp the whole of what I was producing. *My Life and Dr. Joyce Brothers* had been the Inferno, *The Society of Friends* was Purgatory—that place where we must work out right and wrong, good and evil—and looming before me, like a height that would have to be scaled, was Paradiso. My subconscious must have known this long before I did, as the title of the last story in the first book was "A Divine Comedy," which now became my title for the projected trilogy. Indeed, although it's unlikely that the three books will ever be published in one volume, that's how I see the whole: as a long short-story cycle about middle America at the fin-de-siècle and the beginning of the new millennium. These paragraphs near the opening of the last story in *The Society of Friends* clarified for me—and the reader, I hope—what the stories were trying to do (the story is titled "Block Party"):

Perhaps you yourself live in, or have visited, the Midwest. Perhaps you yourself live in, or have visited, a small midwestern town that has burst out of its skin, wandered aimlessly off the beaten track, and fetched up—out of breath, slightly hysterical—in a mall. This modern Middle America is more medieval than it knows; it is Bosch in a baseball cap, Dante in denim. Here there are long summer afternoons when daylight saving seems a sort of forgiveness, seems something that really does save us—for a little while, at least—from death. For, toward evening, the traffic, noisy beyond belief, slows. Speed bicyclists, avenging furies who see their job in life as one of menacing both drivers and pedestrians, go home to strip off spandex shorts from buns of steel before standing under energy-saver showerheads. . . .The fire engines, ambulances, jet planes, hospital helicopter, buses, RVs, and trucks (tree-trimming, garbage, recycling, utility, interstate) all quiet down for an hour or two, although each year they quiet down less, and for a shorter period of time. The sky, pale as a scar, deepens to true blue. Reds rush in—pink, peach, cherry, scarlet, and magenta. As if the wound has been reopened! Then it heals itself, as the stars appear, like stitches, and finally the dark blue of silence enters and erases an entire history of pain.

Perhaps this dark blue silence is like codeine or morphine. Perhaps eternity is a drug, an anesthetic. A numbness that lasts forever.

A tranquilizer that makes you really, really tranquil.

In this town, there will be events to mark births and marriages and deaths. There will be graduation parties and retirement parties. People will enter your life, but some of them will stay in it and others will merely visit for a longer or shorter weekend. Sometimes when you wake on summer mornings, you will remember those who have left and wonder where they are now—returned to cosmic dust, some of them, or drinking cappuccino with a new wife in another state.

There will be block parties.

That is a description that, to use the word again, turns interior. It expresses a feeling—the feeling of the place, as it were. F. Scott Fitzgerald, in *The Great Gatsby*, gives us this superb description of Wisconsin in winter:

When we pulled out into the winter night and the real snow, our snow, began to stretch out beside us and twinkle against the windows, and the dim lights of small Wisconsin stations moved by, a sharp wild brace came suddenly into the air. We drew in deep breaths of it as we walked back from dinner through the cold vestibules, unutterably aware of our identity with this country for one strange hour, before we melted indistinguishably into it again.

That's my Middle West. . .

Reading it, we can feel the damp cold seeping into the train, especially the vestibules between cars, and we see the faint notes of light that might be said to play a song as the train travels through the countryside. But we also have a sense of how the characters feel, how much the Midwest means to them, and we understand that it is the train that permits them to understand, for an hour, how much of the Midwest is in them, how, everywhere they go, they will carry the Midwest with them. The well-made exterior place in fiction must lead to the interior if it is to amount to anything more than mere description.

When Welty called place "one of the lesser angels," she mentioned some of the more important ones: "character, plot, symbolic meaning. . . and feeling, who in my eyes carries the crown, soars highest of them all and rightly relegates place into the shade." I would call feeling an *interior* place. And I would put thinking there, too. How we feel has much to do with how we think, and how we think has much to do with how we feel. Perhaps we can sum them both up as aspects of consciousness, which, of course, includes subconsciousness.

It is possible to write only about the exterior. Hemingway did it in "Hills like White Elephants." The reader of "Hills like White Elephants" has to figure out what the story is about, and even when she does, she has to supply the emotion that is left outside the story, in the margins. He gives us a powerful experience this way, but as a writer I am more interested in what goes on in the minds and hearts of my characters. I want to reach the interior.

Rubin, although he acknowledges that certain writers work best when they feel saturated with the geographical and historical details of a place, of his own work says, "I wrote my own three novels with a city map and a chart of Charleston harbor close by.

In retrospect I believe that what I should have used instead was a stethoscope."

❦

"The good novel," Welty says, contains "all the burden of communicating that initial, spontaneous, overwhelming, driving charge of personal inner feeling that was the novel's reason for being." With which I agree, except that I would make that "personal inner feeling *and thinking*." And I suspect that Welty might have included thinking, too—look at a story like "The Still Moment," a brilliant philosophical investigation in which three men, James Audubon, the Methodist preacher Lorenzo Dow, and the murderer Murrell, each with his own distinct relation to time, are brought to the same temporal point—but felt that to say so might distract the reader from the impact of the story, which must be emotional. "Human life," Welty says, "is fiction's only theme."

But human life includes both feeling and thinking. So let's say that the interior place of consciousness includes both feeling and thinking, and no doubt, writers who target the interior in their work, and that means most of them, tend to emphasize feeling. But there *are* writers who emphasize thinking, and I believe I am one. We are not, alas, the writers who have early successes, because our own lives are so interior that we fail to pay very close attention to the exterior world. Certainly I did. Until I was thirty I couldn't bear to be parted from a book for ten minutes and took one with me wherever I went, stumbling over curbs and walking into parking meters. I conversed, and watched movies, and went to lectures, but to waste the time between one and another by not reading would have been beyond me. Not long ago, as my husband and I were making plans to renovate our barn, he was astonished to learn that I had no idea what Sheetrock is. "You don't get out a lot, do you," he said. Thank goodness, it finally dawned on me that writing *arrived at* thinking and feeling by encompassing a world outside my *own* brain. I needed to observe the external. I also needed to observe *other* brains. "Making reality real," Welty says, "is art's responsibility." Art directs our attention; it populates the world with characters who have inner lives and moral dimension and ethical questions.

Saying nothing about her own work, work that surely is genius, Welty asks how place, as a locus of feeling, affects literary genius. "It may be that place can focus the gigantic, voracious eye of genius and bring its gaze to point. Focus then means awareness, discernment, order, clarity, insight—they are like the attributes of love." I think that's important, that she says they are "like the attributes of love." One of the things I said in my second novel, *Augusta Played*, is that to love is to pay attention. A writer must pay attention. A writer must pay attention to the world she is creating in her work. She must love that world. By the way, love, so defined, is not only not sentimental, it is the opposite of sentimentality.

I have tried to write about Madison with that kind of love. But now I wonder: Am I writing about Madison, or am I writing about much larger place—a *space*—with a nod to Dante.

What interests me most as a writer, it seems, is still the world of the brain, and that includes metaphysics as well as physics. I've made a tentative start to my Paradiso, which will not, of course, be called that, but another group of stories has intervened.

These are stories set in the South. They began to appear when I returned to the South. But when I refer to them as "my southern stories," my husband, who grew up in North Carolina and Virginia and can talk country with any good ol' boy, says, "There's nothing southern about them." The stories take place in Virginia, Tennessee, Alabama, Arkansas, Mississippi, Louisiana, Florida, Texas, and South and North Carolina, but he's right. The stories mention Spanish moss and live oak, sweet tea and po' boy sandwiches, guns and hound dogs—and still they aren't southern. The sun in them fries eggs on sidewalks and still they aren't southern. The characters don't sound southern, not even when I make them speak without apostrophes.

And yet I remember hot nights when moths beat their tiny, mothy brains out on the lampshade. I know what it's like to sweat so much that you can't put a piece of paper into the typewriter without getting it wet. I remember what it was like to listen to the katydids and cicadas and spring peepers in concert with my parents' low voices as they sat on the back patio with friends, sipping highballs. Why can't I get these things into the stories?

I grew up hearing stories about my southern forebears and my parents' childhoods in the Deep South. Why can't I get that stuff into the stories?

When my husband and I pulled out from Madison in the rented moving van and headed south, the South began to return to me, state by state. When I smelled wisteria and magnolia and saw the wide gardens, the denser trees, and, it's true, the cars on cinderblock, I knew I was home. Why can't I get it into my stories?

I've begun to suspect the problem may not be me, that it may even be the South. The South isn't terribly southern these days. People in the South read *The New York Times*. They do consumer research on the Internet before they buy. They eat and shop at the same franchises that can be found in the North, East, and West. Cities have grown, and cable is, if not everywhere, not far away wherever you are. And satellite is better.

To find the old South you have to hang out at a country filling station, or join the Junior League. But even filling stations sell *USA Today*, and the Good Ol' Gals of the Junior League get Botox injections and do yoga or Pilates. A good many southern writers today write about exactly this: the New South emerging in the Old South. Bobbie Ann Mason, with her low-income, individualist characters, and Mary Ward Brown, with her genteel elderly men and women, black and white, trying to live peaceably with an impatient, pressing younger generation, are exemplars of this kind of fiction. Two of my favorite African American writers, Edward P. Jones and ZZ Packer, give us contemporary black life, Packer in her clear-as-water tales of cultured and acculturated black youth and Jones in his stories about black ghetto life in D.C.

Maybe what I'm writing about, then, is a New South. Here is a passage from the Louisiana story. (Connie is Constantine, the unemployed poet with whom Calista lives in an apartment above the store she inherited.)

Calista tried to speak with Connie about how tight money was. "Nobody is buying earrings these days," she said. "Nobody wants their palms read. They're into crystals."

"What will you do?" he asked.

She took a night job waiting tables in a diner. She pulled down the iron grilles over the shop windows and the blind over the door. As soon as she stepped out of the store, the heat hit her like a fist. With each breath she drew she felt as if she were swallowing a cotton ball; in no time, her chest felt stuffed with cotton. Even at six P.M. it was still so hot, the sidewalks smoking with the sunshine that burned into them all day long, that on her way to work she passed a dog weaving in and out of pedestrian traffic, panting and blank-eyed and looking about to keel over from heat stroke. For sure, she said to herself, *dog daze.* "Grab him, Tee-Jay," a boy yelled, and a second boy, as black as if he'd been charred by the same fire of weather, seized the dog by the collar. "I got him, Flagpole!" Tee-Jay crowed. Tee-Jay picked the dog up and gently set him in a round aluminum bucket under a hydrant and Flagpole turned the water on.

Lucky dog.

When the dog was sitting comfortably in this portable swimming pool, the boys petted him on his head and shoulders. "Good ol' dog," they said, in a crooning way. "Good ol' dog."

She had been worried about the dog and relieved when the boys came to his rescue, and she waited until she was sure the dog would be fine and, pushing past dockhands, drag queens, and tourists, she was still late to work and to make up for being late kept her mind on the job and never even glanced out the windows. She didn't see the sun set and barely noticed when the lights

THE GLOBE AND THE BRAIN: ON PLACE IN FICTION   167

in the diner came on. When she got home at two A.M.,
she found a poem on her pillow and carried it into the
bathroom to read:
>the night is dark
>i cannot see
>i cannot feel
>i cannot touch
>i can only hear
>the stars falling
>out of the sky,
>landing at my feet
>with a loud *ker-plop*

Taking her uniform off in the dark, lying down na-
ked beside him, Calista imagined *stars falling out of the
sky, landing* at the foot of the bed, but, landing not on
a field somewhere but on a tile floor, going *donk-donk-
donk* instead of *ker-plop*, metallic-sounding at first, like
lilliputian space ships, space ships the size of actual
cup saucers, but then burning out with a small hiss.
So actually, she thought, the sound would be more like
donkss-donkss-donkss. She wanted to point this out to
Constantine, but he was asleep, and besides, he was the
poet.

Then again, *Faulkner* wrote about how the South was changing. A place changes, and writers take note of the changes. When
was this not true?

Someone might reasonably ask why I don't just move my
"southern stories" elsewhere. Well, for one thing, each protagonist (they are all women in this group) appeared in my imagination already attached to a southern state. For another, the
stories are *about* the South even if they are not southern. These
women, not one of whom is in any way a projection of myself,
nevertheless seem real to me, as if I know them, as if I have always known them, so maybe the women, if not the stories, are
somehow southern. Finally, you may be familiar with the Dead

Mule Theory of Southern Fiction, which states that in every le-
gitimately southern book there will be a dead mule? To make my
stories qualify, I have stuck a dead mule into one of them.

In the end, they are what they are—or I should say, since I
haven't finished them, they will be what they will be, and what
that will be, will be for readers to say, not me. Someone might
ask why I should care whether I'm thought of as a southern writer. Maybe I'm *not* a southern writer. But I would love to have a
southern audience, because southern readers cherish their literary heritage and honor—and feel themselves in relation with—
southern writers. It seems to me that the Northwest, starting
later, is creating a similar tradition, a cultural environment in
which writers and readers are reciprocally responsive. Wallace
Stegner said that "[e]xcept in northern California, the West has
never had a real literary outpouring, a flowering of the sort that
marked New England, the Midwest, and the South.... [A] lot of
what has been written is a literature of motion, not of place...
from Mark Twain's *Roughing It* to Kerouac's *On the Road*." But
I think there is a plethora of small-press activity that indicates
the Northwest moment is either now or very near. Writers like
Richard Hugo, Theodore Roethke, Carolyn Kizer, Raymond
Carver, Ken Kesey, Norman Maclean, Tom Robbins, Richard
Brautigan, and Jack Cady have forged a foundation. *The Idaho
Review*, out of Boise, is a first-class literary annual. *The Seattle
Review* is a great place for writing students to learn how to se-
lect and edit writing and a good place to publish. Washington,
Montana, Oregon, Vancouver, northern California are all active
literary sites. This kind of environment is a wonderful privilege
for a writer: it takes the edge off the isolation of the writerly life
and encourages the writer to address the world around her.

Which, as Welty reminds us, is local. "It is by the nature of
itself that fiction is all bound up in the local," she says. She calls
it "the heart's field."

So maybe, nowadays, the local is becoming the global. This
may be one reason so much of literature in America today is
about India or China or Alaska: we relish the diversity of cul-
tures and histories and want to know them as well as we can

before they are lost in a state of amalgamation. Yet if this seems depressing—the thought that in a few more centuries every place on earth will be pretty much like every other place on earth—by that time we may be able to see our planet as local. Against the black backdrop of outer space, our blue and green earth, so small, so beautiful, may be valued for what it is: our home.

In the meantime, every writer's work contributes to Stegner's coral reef. Even as the writer looks to anchor her work to place, her work provides that place with a sense of itself. The relation is symbiotic, and over time it can become difficult to distinguish between the place and what has been written about it. Elizabethan England *is* Shakespeare, Ben Jonson, Marlowe. Suburban nineteenth-century France *is* Flaubert. The South *is* Faulkner, Welty, Flannery O'Connor, George Garrett, Elizabeth Spencer, Chappell, Lee Smith, Henry Taylor, Ellen Gilchrist, Kaye Gibbons, Dave Smith, R. H. W. Dillard, and an amazing number of other writers. As Stegner puts it, "No place is a place until things that have happened in it are remembered in history, ballads, yarns, legends, or monuments. Fictions serve as well as facts." Or one might say that art and reality are in cahoots, each serving the other.

WHAT COMES NEXT: WOMEN WRITING WOMEN IN CONTEMPORARY SHORT FICTION

There must be trends in contemporary short fiction by women, but exactly what those trends are may be almost impossible to say, or at least very difficult for a woman writer to say, the same way it is difficult for anyone to fathom, in a mirror, the visual impression her or his own face makes. You look into a mirror, and you see the person you once were, or the person you imagine others think you are, or the person you have never been but wished to be, or that person you have, always, recognized yourself as being and yet hoped against hope no one else could see. You almost never see who you are now, today, this stranger scrutinizing a reflection as if it might be, somehow, more real than the self engaged in reflecting.

One thing, however, is clear, does offer itself up to reflection: The first thing to be said about women writers of short fiction today is that there are *more* of them than there were. There are many more than there were even just a short while ago. In the United States, this is partly because there are more short story writers of both sexes than there used to be. Our academic system of undergraduate English majors with a creative writing emphasis followed by Master of Fine Arts programs utilizing the workshop method of analysis and criticism has contributed to a mushrooming (if not necessarily a flowering) of short fiction. Short stories are, after all, short; they can be read and discussed in the span of a two- or three-hour workshop as novels cannot. The short story form may daunt the novice writer less than does the novel, which, generally at least, requires a commitment of several years and a narrative ability that seems to bear some relation, if not an absolute relation, to experience and wisdom. At the same time, the short story's traditional inclination toward epiphany, its formal belief in enlightenment and resolution, draws the young writer as irresistibly as any promise of fulfillment. The short story says to the young writer, *I can be completed, I can fulfill you, happiness is within your grasp.* (The older writer, of course, knows that love is fickle, even the love of an art form for an artist, and that, as with all relationships, the only fulfillment is found, oddly, in an endless giving of the self.)

So it is that, even in an era of shrinking markets—when a magazine like *Mademoiselle* ends its quite glorious heritage of fifty-seven years of publishing serious fiction; when *Redbook*, which had published, among its pages of advice for young mothers, the work of some of the best writers, men and women, around, admits that it now prefers popular fiction—even at this time more writers are writing more short stories than ever before, publishing, if not in slick magazines, then in academic and literary journals such as *The Georgia Review, Fiction, The Gettysburg Review, The Greensboro Review* . . . a list far too long even to begin. And so it is that many of these writers of short stories are women.

I published my first book, a novel, in 1974. I had previously published four or five short stories with enough success to gratify a young writer, but my first attraction was to long forms. My *very* first attraction was to long poetry. The first serious poem I ever attempted—I was sixteen or seventeen—echoed *The Waste Land,* as perhaps everything written by a young poet in those days did, and sustained itself for some pages. It was titled *Heatherland*, and it was naturally about a young woman—*girl*, we said then—named Heather: an instance of the young poet looking for herself in a mirror.

But my interest in long forms was honestly come by, as I had grown up with parents who were string quartet violinists and who particularly loved the late Beethoven quartets. I had grown up loving that music myself; and there is no art more interested in problems of development than the Beethoven string quartets.

In 1974, then, when I published my first book it was a novel, not a collection of short stories. I didn't know any other women fiction writers my own age, although I had read some of what I thought of as the older generation: Mary McCarthy, Katherine Anne Porter, Flannery O'Connor. I had read, of contemporary overseas fiction writers who were women, Iris Murdoch and Muriel Spark, Beryl Bainbridge, a few others. And I had read a young American poet named Erica Jong whose first novel, *Fear of Flying*, had been published just a year earlier. It was difficult for a young woman writer to get published, and if she managed it she might, like Erica Jong, be praised by John Updike in *The New Yorker*, but the praise would be for her "bawdiness" and, as I remember, anyway, her white teeth, which he had apparently found exceedingly mesmerizing in the jacket photograph. I hasten to add that I did not feel disinherited, exactly, by the tradition of men writers, whose works I read as or more avidly, but I did feel a need to prove something—my claim on that heritage, my worthiness—and perhaps I had been disinherited, without knowing it.

Ms. magazine started up not long before this, and while I was in full sympathy with its feminist goals of achieving equality of opportunity and pay for women, I was less enthralled with its cultural agenda, which derived, I believe, from a confusion of fiction with propaganda that still bollixes critical treatment of fiction by women. Identifying the patriarchal with the hierarchical, *Ms.*, in those early, understandably defensive, days, decided to have a "review committee" rather than a book editor. The review of my first novel had come in and was so praiseful, and so firmly scheduled, that copy was sent to my publisher, who forwarded it to me. Alas, the review committee then fell to arguing about the ending of my book. In the last chapter my heroine agreed to *transfer from one medical school to another* in order to be near her boyfriend. Some members of the committee thought that to change schools for reasons of love was inexcusably antifeminist—in my eyes the heroine was growing as a person by being willing to commit herself to another—and the review was killed.

Ten years later, for my fourth novel and sixth book, I did receive a lovely review from *Ms.*, though I don't know whether they were still doing things by committee. Perhaps this review represented just one voice (but I'm fond of *Ms.* and like to think an entire committee voted to return my feeling). Interestingly enough, the book, The *Lost Traveller's Dream*, was one I had intended to be a book of short stories. The stories were interlinked but only in a strange sort of way, as those in the second section were told by a narrator who was the creation of the narrator of the first section; the narrator of the third section was then revealed as the creator of the narrator of the first section. There was this ontological interlinkage, but no narrative progression tied the three sections together and so I thought of the book as a collection of stories.

In 1984 the vogue for book collections of short stories was just beginning to pick up speed, but my editor still cleaved to the accepted publishing wisdom regarding collections of short stories; namely, that they did not sell. He tried to talk me into calling the book a novel; I balked, but I agreed to sign a contract calling the book a collection of three novellas. Sad to say, I lacked the courage of my conviction, feeling a need to achieve a wider readership, and as the editing process got underway I found myself giving in and adding material to make the book something more like a novel. The result still embarrasses me, and I hope someday to have an opportunity to revise it in the direction of my original vision.

Meanwhile, the accepted publishing wisdom, it turned out, had just gone out the window: suddenly short story collections *were* selling. A young woman named Pam Houston hit the bestseller list in the early nineties with a first collection (and first book) of finely tuned stories titled, enchantingly, *Cowboys Are My Weakness.* The paperback rights to this book sold for a cheeringly large sum, reminding us that at least once in a while artistic virtue needn't be its own reward, or its only reward. If other collections did not sell in great numbers, they sold steadily, presumably often to other young writers.

Most story writers, as we know, will continue to get two free copies of the magazine in which their work appears; my point here is not that stories are earning more money than they used to (they are not) but that more of them are being written by women.

Until recently, the great triumvirate of women short story writers in the States today was made up of Eudora Welty, Grace Paley (both now deceased) and Cynthia Ozick; these three writers formed a constellation that is a collective shining light for any woman writer of short fiction. (Elizabeth Spencer, fully their equal, is better known for her novels.) Welty is lauded for her inimitable talent for characterization, as in her story "The Worn Path," for her ability to render an entire world in the brief span of a story. She created a body of work that serves as inspiration and validation for quite a few younger writers, including Lee Smith, Jill McCorkle, and Bobbie Ann Mason. Her astounding ability to unveil the soul of the "Other," as in "A Worn Path"'s portrait of an elderly black woman, Phoenix Jackson, walking to the doctor's office for medicine for her grandson, proves once and for all that a woman writer is not imprisoned by self, is not confined by boundaries of biology to the subjective, the autobiographical. Welty is also one of the major stylists of the twentieth century, although she may not be recognized as such because her use of language is never self-reflexive, never in service to an image of the author. From beautiful, clear, precise description of the natural world to stunningly decentered rhythms conveying psychological intensity, her attempt is not to prettify but to approach truth as closely as possible. Consider, too, a sentence such as this one from her story "Why I Live at the P.O.": "Papa-Daddy's Mama's

papa and sulks." In my estimation, a writer who wrote that
sentence would laugh all day long, and the next day, too, and
have a right to. Paley's urban rhythms, her bold dislocation of
structural and even grammatical convention that conveys modern
speech patterns and modern-life patterns so naturally that the
reader forgets the formal radicalism that parallels her political
radicalism, create a marvelous music. Ozick may be accurately
called—she would probably dislike this shorthand, disliking
any formulaic phrase, and yet the phrase will be meaningful
to readers who may not yet have read her work—"the Flannery
O'Connor of Jewish literature," sublimely identified by her wry
and penetrating intelligence and her gift for concentrating it on
thorny subjects of moral and spiritual resonance.

Born in 1928, Ozick belongs to a generation that came to the
age of conscience and consciousness during World War II, and
much of her work has been dedicated to an attempt to comprehend
or, if that's not possible—to comprehend the incomprehensible—
at least to remember, the horror of the Holocaust. In her story
"The Shawl," Rosa, a mother nursing her child, and her niece,
Stella, are force-marched to a camp. Rosa's milk dries up, and the
baby, Magda, sucks on Rosa's shawl, a "milk of linen." The shawl
hides Magda, allowing her to be mistaken for Rosa's breasts. But
then Magda learns to walk. She even laughs, though it is a silent
laugh. She is life, growing and becoming itself, there in the death-
camp. She has survived this long—fifteen months—because she
is, thinks Rosa, mute. But the niece, Stella, fourteen years old
and desperate to live too, takes the shawl away from Magda,
and Magda—this is inevitable, this is circumstance, this is the
inevitable circumstance that is tragedy—cries. She bursts into a
huge howling. Rosa rushes to get the shawl, but she returns only
in time to see Magda carried off by a guard and then hurled at the
electric fence. Rosa

> only stood, because if she ran they would shoot, and
> if she tried to pick up the sticks of Magda's body they
> would shoot, and if she let the wolf's screech ascending
> now through the ladder of her skeleton break out, they

would shoot; so she took Magda's shawl and filled her own mouth with it, stuffed it in and stuffed it in, until she was swallowing up the wolf's screech and tasting the cinnamon and almond depth of Magda's saliva; and Rosa drank Magda's shawl until it dried.

There is a connection here, a connection between speech and motherhood, that may be emblematic of what many women writers are doing today, whether their subjects are as extreme as Ozick's or as mild, even, one might say, as depressed, as some of the minimalists'. Perhaps women, having been mistaught for so long that their creative energy is drained by the process they go through to become women, have figured out that what was so draining was not psychical formation but having to hold down a job, run a household, and raise children. It is of some help at least to know who the enemy is, and the enemy is not gender *per se* but economics.

Poor Rosa literally swallows her own grief; in this story, she cannot speak. But the story itself is a shriek, a howl like Magda's, a single, drawn-out, piercing cry; the author makes her voice heard.

Grace Paley, in a story titled "Mother" barely longer than one page, gives us the reverse lamentation, the daughter feeling the loss of her mother. The story begins: "One day I was listening to the AM radio. I heard a song: 'Oh, I Long to See My Mother in the Doorway.' By God! I said, I understand that song. I have often longed to see my mother in the doorway. As a matter of fact, she did stand frequently in various doorways looking at me." Echoing the three-times rituals of fairytales, the narrator then recalls three times when her mother stood in the door. "She stood one day, just so, at the front door, the darkness of the hallway behind her. It was New Year's Day. She said sadly, If you come home at 4 A.M. when you're seventeen, what time will you come home when you're twenty?" The narrator's second memory is of her mother at the entrance to her daughter's room at home. "I had just issued a political manifesto attacking the family's position on the Soviet Union. She said, Go to sleep for godsakes, you damn fool, you and your Communist ideas. We saw them already, Papa and me, in 1905." And then the third memory: "At the door of the kitchen she said, You never finish your lunch. You run around senselessly. What will become of you?"

"Then," the narrator says, "she died."

Importantly, that is not a punch line. The story continues, conjuring the narrator's parents in their living room. In the middle of the mother's bid to get her husband to open up, to talk to her, the narrator admits that she wishes she could see her mother "in the doorway of the living room." But this cannot happen, and the father says he is too tired to talk.

"Then she died."

The repetition of the statement "Then she died" resonates with shock. The narrator cannot, even now, accept that her mother is gone, that so much went unsaid. It is the repetition that persuades us we are hearing more than a writer's voice, that we are hearing the voice of a narrator whose feeling is genuine and deep.

The narrator's mother dies still wanting to be talked to a little. Such a gulf that has opened up between the father and the mother! Such a sense of lost opportunities for closeness we feel reading this story, of missed humanity! And yet Paley manages to make us feel, too, the father's weariness with the dark side of life. And we feel that this man and woman know how to accommodate each other even if they do not know each other fully. But the daughter, we feel, failed to accommodate her mother when she had the chance. Perhaps the story is a way of talking to her mother a little.

"Write to me," the widowed mother tells her daughter in a story by a younger writer, Jayne Anne Phillips. "You seem so far away." The story, "Souvenir," recounts the daughter's response to her mother's illness. After the mother is operated on for a brain tumor, Kate spends time at the hospital with her. The mother wonders about her own future. "I wonder where I'm headed," she says, and Kate responds, "I want you right here to see me settle down into normal American womanhood."

But "normal American womanhood" is not a comfortable condition in most contemporary stories. The writer Helen Schulman, who has since published novels, has written a story titled "Pushing the Point" about the competitive friendship between a tough-on-the-outside "leatherette" sixteen-year-old named Rhonda and a same-age narrator who says, "I am bad. She's badder." Schulman's language is a burnished slang; she takes street-talk and spins it so tightly into itself, the twist-and-shout of itself, that the slanginess of it disappears, a Rumpelstiltskin prose. The two girls have been hanging out in a bar, looking for action; Rhonda has found it. The narrator thinks:

Now I am lit. Boozing rock and rolls me. I go to the juke; I hustle up some change. But the tunes are beat; college stuff, this place drives me crazy. I even had to pull out the fake I.D. to get in past the door. I used Rhonda's forged nurse's badge because bouncers never card her. Most times when we're out together they don't bother me. Everything looks older when it's next to Rhonda.

I scope. While I wait on her I'd like for some guy to cough it up and buy me another drink. But college kids come in couples, two by two; they've ark'd out an entire wall. And then there's that bunch of droolers in the corner. One of them starts with me but I freeze-dry him; my eyes blast out a shock of cold. I move. I boogie to this city jive, and as I spin away from him I see Rhonda's reflection steaming up the glass door.

She's back. She pulls me over. There are sweat beads glittering in the hollows of her throat. "We did it in a lobby," says Rhonda.

Later the narrator drives home, somewhat the worse for wear.

The rain hits the line and yellow splashes up my Converse. It hits the car lights and they run. Streetlights wax down on either side of me: everything melts if you push it to its point.

The splendid African American writer Colleen J. McElroy describes a similar character in her story "Imogene," included in her book *Jesus and Fat Tuesday*, a collection that covers nearly a hundred years of black history without ever making a show of its own ambition. But Imogene is a softer character. She believes she's in love. She thinks she must be drawn to him, the man she is sure she loves, for his style, the way he walks and dresses. Or no, she thinks: "It was the touching." Or maybe, "It was the way he tilted his head." His hands, his thighs. The reader is beginning to realize that this gorgeous creature is nowhere in sight. Imogene is hunting for him in the San Francisco night. "*The good looking ones run faster*, she thought." She stops in a bar, the Tambourine. She'll have a drink. She decides to make it a double.

And he's there. She joins him at his table. He suggests that they go for a walk. She hesitates, then tells herself that he waited for her.

She follows him to a car. He opens the door, gives her to a "Mr. Preston." He reminds her to get fifty bucks. He says he'll be in the bar. He leaves her there.

The man in the car starts to take what he's paying for, but Imogene is thinking of the one she loves. The story closes, "But her thoughts were clear: she remembered her man, how he had smiled and the warm feeling when his hands brushed her face just before she'd slid into the car and the door had closed. She hoped he would be in a good mood when she got back to the Tambourine. Her sweater fell open and she let her body go soft, leaning into the seat, stroking the smooth leather with her free hand."

Many of these women, one begins to think, are trapped by sex, *in* sex. Joyce Carol Oates's well-known story "Where Are You Going, Where Have You Been?" presents a fifteen-year-old, Connie, who is, we realize, trapped forever. Enormous, almost suffocating tension builds as the reader sees Connie—a girl who is only a tiny bit daring, a girl who doesn't, not really, do anything "wrong"—becoming fatally entrapped by the psychotic Arnold Friend. Her family have gone to a barbecue, leaving her at home alone. Arnold and his sidekick have been watching her and know she is alone. She knows she's in trouble; she wants to get away from it—this destiny that has abruptly manifested itself to her as hers—but there is no way she can. "We'll go out to a nice field," Arnold tells her, "out in the country here where it smells so nice and it's sunny." She is caught in an eternal darkness, on a bright summer day that cannot end.

Usually the entrapment is metaphorical. In the title story of her second collection, *Lust*, Susan Minot, one of the minimalists who came on the scene in the mid-eighties accompanied by much marketing hoopla—gives us a young woman whose inner life is so claustrophobically unvarious that she seems to consider the boys she knows solely in terms of their sexual attributes. In short staccato paragraphs, we get a series of sexual descriptions:

Leo was from a long time ago, the first one I ever saw nude. In the spring before the Hellmans filled their pool, we'd go down there in the deep end, with baby oil, and like that. I met him the first month away at boarding school. He had a halo from the campus light behind him. I flipped.

Roger was fast. In his illegal car, we drove to the reservoir, the radio blaring, talking fast, fast, fast. He was always going for my zipper. He got kicked out sophomore year.

By the time the band got around to playing "Wild Horses," I had tasted Bruce's tongue. We were clicking in the shadows on the other side of the amplifier, out of Mrs. Donovan's line of vision. It tasted like salt, with my neck bent back, because we had been dancing so hard before.

We are meant to sympathize with a youthful narrator whose privileged but neglectful upbringing has left her without direction, without self-respect, without the love of the boys she sleeps with. "After the briskness of loving," says the narrator, "loving stops. . . .You seem to have disappeared." The language, flat, uninflected, is a mirror of a despair so deep it goes beyond the narrator's ability to understand it for herself. Fiction writers Christine Schutt, Dawn Raffel, and A. Manette Ansay also play with language in fierce and surprising, often unsettling, ways. Another of the minimalists is Amy Hempel, who, if she never wrote another story, could consider that she had accomplished a significant achievement with a piece called "In the Cemetery Where Al Jolson Is Buried." Here, the minimalist impulse to pull back from drama, to downplay crisis and steer clear of comment, to *stay cool*, clarifies the immense pain the narrator experiences when her best friend dies. The concluding image of the story is of a chimp who had been taught sign language by research psychologists:

> In the course of the experiment, that chimp had a baby. Imagine how her trainers must have thrilled when the mother, without prompting, began to sign to the newborn. Baby, drink milk. Baby, play ball. And when the baby died, the mother stood over the body, her wrinkled hands moving with animal grace, forming again and again the words, Baby, come hug, Baby, come hug, fluent now in the language of grief.

Not all short stories by younger women writers today are written in "the language of grief"—though, to be sure, many are, as if to be young is necessarily, even in these muddled times, to be as yet unreconciled to loss, to be passionate about injustice. While I have tried not to cross the line into Canada (because I don't feel qualified to have opinions about Canadian fiction *qua* Canadian fiction), I have to adduce here the Canadian writer Barbara Gowdy. Of her several books of fiction, I wish to mention particularly her third book. *We So Seldom Look on Love* is extraordinary—original, daring. In eight stories narrated in the first or third person, Gowdy pulls us so quickly into the lives of characters that we are there before we know it and are already happily ensconced when we learn that where we are is in the life (or lives) of a two-headed man, or Siamese twins named Sylvie and Sue, or foster children who are blind or epileptic, or children who are hydrocephalic or hyperactive, or a wife who exhibits herself in the nude, daily, for a voyeur in a neighboring building. Or a woman whose child has been decapitated by a ceiling fan.

In the title story, a young woman makes necrophilic love at the funeral home where she has a part-time job. I never thought that I would find a story about necrophilia sweet, funny, or charming, but this story is sweet, and funny, and charming. Also shrewd: "I think that all desire is desire for transformation," the narrator asserts, "and that all transformation—all movement, all process—happens because life turns into death."

In fact, several of these stories have more going on in them than many a novel. In the last and longest story, "Flesh of My Flesh," Marion, who was nineteen when her mother was murdered, learns that her new husband, Sam, is a woman who has been taking hormones to prepare for the final physical transformation into a man. "She starts to cry. . . .She buries her face in the pillow so that Sam won't hear. She wants her mother. *She* knows better, but year after year her heart goes on pumping out love as if all it knows is circulation. . . ."

Even more amazing than the artful narrative structures by which Gowdy involves the reader are the warmth and good humor and energetic intelligence of her characters—and there is a range of characters here, the protagonists, for all their seeming oddity, being fully developed socially as well as psychologically, so that they exist in a network of relatives and friends of widely varying ages and attitudes. Gowdy convinces us that people who may be said to have crossed "a vast behavioural gulf" are not very different from those who remain on one side. She also convinces us that all of us, at some point, cross that gulf. Here are eight stories so surgically painful and precise as to drill a hole in the reader's heart. Yet it is a healing operation, leading to an enlarged, embracing sense of life. This is fiction that vivifies. Short fiction by women has as many tones and timbres as an orchestra. No rule of gender restricts the woman writer to lamentation, rage, or whispers of despair. The Chicana writer Sandra Cisneros— who cuts a rather dashing figure in bicycle shorts and a colorful top, I can testify, having gone to hear her give a reading not long ago—pens an affectionate riff on family in "Hairs," wherein each member of the narrator's family has his or her hair described. "And me," she writes, "my hair is lazy. It never obeys barrettes or bands." But it is her mother's hair that is "sweet to put your nose into when she is holding you."

We are back with mothers, it seems, mothers and daughters. Not the only theme of contemporary fiction by women, obviously, but a large one, as if women writers were, in a new way now, self-consciously working toward a sense of literary tradition as a heritage, a thing that belongs to them and to which they belong. T. S. Eliot made a point of saying—and too many feminist literary theorists (I say this as a feminist) have forgotten that he said this—that tradition

> cannot be inherited, and if you want it you must obtain it by great labour. It involves, in the first place, the historical sense . . . and the historical sense involves a perception, not only of the pastness of the past, but of its presence; the historical sense compels a man to write not merely with his own generation in his bones, but with a feeling that the whole of the literature of Europe from Homer and within it the whole of the literature of his own country has a simultaneous existence and composes a simultaneous order.

But T. S. Eliot, the author of that poem that had so moved me when I was a teenager that I recited the ending to myself as I crossed campus, a private transportation, could write as he did about tradition precisely because he *did* assume that the tradition of, as he puts it, "the whole of the literature of Europe" was waiting for him to claim it as his legacy. Women writers may believe that a tradition must be obtained with an even greater labor than Eliot thought, that, indeed, before it can be claimed it must be created. We are writing ourselves into existence as our own literary mothers; we will become our literary daughters; the place settings we are handing down we have, let us not forget, hammered out in the silversmithy of our own souls.

In an essay titled "The Parable of the Cave or: In Praise of Watercolors," Mary Gordon describes how she was brought up to be "a good girl," a daughter who reflected her father's image. She still credits her father for encouraging her to write, but, she says, "now I see that I am the *kind* of writer I am because I am my mother's daughter. My father's tastes ran to the metaphysical. My mother taught me to listen to conversations at the dinner table; she taught me to remember jokes." She continues, "My subject as a writer has far more to do with family happiness than with the music of the spheres."

My mother, bless her, loved the music of the spheres, loved it as deeply and as unsentimentally as my father did, and if she was short on other kinds of love she had that love to give me and did. I understand what Gordon is saying—that we need to attend to the quieter, less cosmic notes—and I quite agree. In two books of interconnected stories, *My Life and Dr. Joyce Brothers* and *The Society of Friends*—I attempt to call attention to those more mundane notes and even to some not previously or often sounded, the underground notes, let's say, of a woman who has had to lead much of her emotional life in secrecy. But I would not want us to cease to hear the music of the spheres, also, nor would I want us to turn over the playing of it only to the men writers. "Something sings in my heart," I wrote in an earlier story set in the Northwest, on the Pacific, a story in *The Lost Traveller's Dream*, where it appears denuded of its title; "I have a canary in my rib cage, and he sings and sings. There's salt on the air, water in my boot, and music everywhere. Sound is pure structure, the plan underlying this liberality of existential stuff, swelling. Three dark rocks rise out of the sea, wet as seals; under a gray sky, the water is as green as grass. When a wave breaks, foam forms first at the outer points and rolls down the wave's length like a prairie catching fire, white fire.... The trick is to shed your soul on the beach like a snakeskin; in that profoundly bare condition, you will be able to tread water like ground, the continental shelf will emerge to support you. Amazingly, the farther out you go, the wider your world becomes; your perspective expands, and forsaking *de facto* being, you achieve the infinite dimensions of the imagination. All things glow; seaweed, clouds, fish are radiant when beheld. The third eye is a tiny Christ nailed to a tiny cross on your forehead, right between the other two."

But I was, as I say, younger then, unreconciled to loss, and passionate about injustice. This is not to say that age must reconcile us to loss or make us any the less passionate about injustice; rather, it is to say that we women who have been writing awhile, not unlike the strengthening tradition itself, have entered a place that is both exotically unfamiliar and hauntingly familiar. Consider the narrator of Grace Paley's story "The Long-Distance Runner," who seizes our attention in her opening sentence by declaring, "One day, before or after forty-two, I became a long-distance runner." And she runs in the country first, and then on the boardwalk, and then to her old neighborhood, where she grew up. She runs to the apartment she used to live in and, fantastically, moves in with the current tenants. When she goes home she tells her family of her adventures. How can she explain this? "A woman inside the steamy energy of middle age runs and runs," she says. "She finds the houses and streets where her childhood happened. She lives in them. She learns as though she was still a child what in the world is coming next."

WHY I WRITE NOW

I was in New York for the week, staying at a hotel that was formerly a flop house but was by then mentioned in see-America-on-a-shoestring travel guides published in Europe, so that French, German, Swedish tourists crowded the lobby. Dialing from a pay phone on the street—to avoid room charges—I telephoned a friend who lived in the city. It was April, and the streets were loud with cars, trucks, messengers on bikes, vendors hawking wares, and pedestrians clomping across intersections, but in tiny square yards about the size of a square yard greenery flourished as if it were growing in a meadow.

My chum was close to fifteen years younger than I, but we were both writers, we were both living the single life, we both wore eye makeup, and we got along well. It was difficult to hear with so much noise in the background, but she gave me directions and when I arrived at her apartment she said, "I have two tickets to the opera. Would you like to go with me?"

Tickets to the Metropolitan Opera—orchestra seats, no less—were beyond my budget and, I'd have thought, hers. She made it clear that she had planned to ask a male friend to join her but that, seeing me in the doorway to her apartment in the meat-packing district, she impulsively asked me. It was a generous gesture.

For the opera we both dressed in, of course, Manhattan black. Her skirt was long, my dress short. All around us swirled the beautiful people in designer clothing. We found our seats, and looking at the rich and famous she asked, "Which would you rather be, unknown in your lifetime but famous after death, or famous now and forgotten later?"

It was not that I had never heard this question before. Every teenager who has ever wanted to write, paint, sculpt, or compose has encountered it. It's almost a rite of passage.

The auditorium lights had blinked in warning; now they dimmed and as they went dark my friend added, "Oh, that's ridiculous! One has to hope for fame in one's own time."

The orchestra plunged into the overture. The curtain rose. I heard and saw nothing. My entire life had just been invalidated.

I had been one of those kids who test themselves with that question. Why did it now upset me so?

I guess: because I was no longer a kid. Fame in my lifetime had ceased to seem something that might someday happen.

For my friend, fame in her lifetime was still a possibility—even, it already seemed, a likelihood. The time I had been born into had changed, and young women writers now received a major publishing push, where before they had been relegated to minor or exceptional positions. There had been Eudora Welty and Mary McCarthy, Katherine Anne Porter and Hannah Arendt, but by and large women writers, until the eighties and nineties, were considered lesser life forms. Nor was circumstance the only reason few people knew my work. All on my own, even without the help of sexism, capitalism, and bad timing, I had managed to make every mistake a writer could make in the commission of her career. I'd left New York City just as my first novel was being published. I'd hooked up with a literary agency without (but I didn't realize it then) credence in the publishing world. Instead of immediately publishing a second novel, I brought out two books of poems. Instead of following up those immediately with a third collection I let eleven years lapse before I published *Natural Theology*. And those are only *examples*.

So I had missed the brass ring. I wasn't even on the merry-go-round. Shoot. I wasn't even at the fair.

I was just writing, with the same blind devotion I had always had.

For posterity? Who knows? Books that receive attention in their own time are more likely to be remembered: there are more copies in libraries (many libraries throw out books that nobody has checked out in a year, or five years); critics and scholars are more likely to write about them. Fame in one's own lifetime might not guarantee fame after death, but it raises the chances.

If there *is* posterity. There might not *be* posterity. An asteroid may wipe out human life, including all the readers. Libraries have been known to burn. Entropy may turn the entire universe, including literature, to soup.

And if entropy seems far-fetched, illiteracy does not. If there is posterity, it could very well be illiterate. Apple icons could supplant the alphabet.

So why not do everything one can to win fame, acclaim, while one can enjoy it?

Sitting there next to my friend, singers vocalizing, I couldn't formulate any of these thoughts. Not yet. Anxiety had shut down my brain. The one thought I had was, *Something is wrong with what she said*. But what?

I had other places to visit after my week in the city, and wherever I went I was nagged by the thought that something had been wrong with what she said, and still I couldn't figure it out.

Because anxiety had narrowed my field of vision, it took me a long time to see the obvious.

One night at a writers' conference I lay in bed recalling that evening at the Met. I heard my friend's words again. Then I sat up and turned on the light. The work, I thought, she left out the work!

Better late than never.

In her equation there had been only two terms: the artist and the audience. If that were all there was to be considered, of course it was only logical to think in terms of the relation between the two. But there was a third term, and it was at least as important as the other two. The third term was the art.

The artist, the audience, and the art.

Faulkner, in his Nobel speech, said he wrote "not for glory and least of all for profit." He said that "the basest of all things is to be afraid," and he worried that the atomic bomb had caused younger writers to turn away from "the old verities and truths of the heart" to a near-sighted focus on the self.

We live in our own time of terror.

Art is more important than the artist. It is even more important than the audience, no matter how elegantly dressed (and wouldn't it be fine if opera gloves came back into fashion). A writer does her best for the work—not for its own sake (I am not speaking of art for art's sake)—but because only if it is coherent, whole, complex, and stable will it endure.

Endure, perhaps, for no one to read. And what is the good of that?

Faulkner believed that man will prevail "because he has a soul, a spirit capable of compassion and sacrifice and endurance." The writer's voice, he said, can "help him endure and prevail." I may be less sanguine than Faulkner but I believe that the human spirit, whether human beings survive or do not, is magnificent and fathomless, breathtaking in its aptitudes for both good and evil, and capable of the most exalted action. It deserves to be recognized for what it is—a transformative power.

I am speaking of art for the sake of the human spirit.

The human spirit survives and prevails in the written word (the well-written word). Literature is testimony and tribute; it upholds our world. When people have gone from the world, literature will still bear witness to the breadth and depth of humanity, of humanness. No—not bear witness to: it will be the human spirit, extant, alive. Our books are us; they will be what we were.

And if the books themselves are lost—burned, or buried

in an avalanche or on purpose to avoid warehouse storage costs, or overwhelmed by melting polar caps? If they are seized and destroyed as contraband? But there is, after all, a limit to how much a writer can worry about.

A writer craves a little fame, a few prizes and more readers, but that is not why she writes. Her deepest concern is not for herself, here or hereafter; her concern, her dream, is to make a thing that does not, cannot, die. So what if it goes unread. Her dream is to create an object of beauty and power that gives to the human spirit a home in eternity. Her dream is to discover the shape and substance of the soul. That shape, that substance: that is the work of art.

III

CALLED TO IT:
AN AUTOBIOGRAPHY

When I start to talk about my parents and their lives as string quartet violinists—which I do whenever I'm asked about my own life, because music and my parents' devotion to it were there from the beginning for me, were what I was born into—listeners are apt to say, "Now we understand why you are so driven." They will sometimes offer up the thought that I see my work as a way to earn my parents' approval, that I hope, by meeting the standards for art set by my parents, to earn their love. This is why I am a perfectionist, they will—they have—told me. I don't argue with them, in part because people rarely want to know more about you than they already do; and in part because the truth involves feelings I have wanted to protect, out of guilt or a fear of embarrassing myself or maybe simply a fear of being wrong. I *could* be wrong, but I do not believe that I am driven. I do not believe I write hoping to win my (now-deceased) parents' love, attention, praise, approval. I believe that if I had wanted to win my late parents' love, attention, praise, approval, I would have said yes to the boy who asked me to the senior prom. I would have gone through sorority rush. I would have learned to dance. I would have learned to cook and garden and play poker. I would have done those things and others like them, because although my parents would not tolerate the almost, the cheap, the untested, the unnecessary in their art, they were not ogres, and when they said that all they wanted from us, the children, was for us to be happy, they meant it. But I had already given my heart to that music I heard while I was still in the womb. I would have heard it anyway—it was what their days were made of—but my mother had read that babies in the womb are influenced by what they hear, and, as if rehearsals and practice sessions and concerts were not enough, she played recordings all through the Louisiana spring and summer and autumn to make *sure* that I heard it, the most beautiful music there is, a music made equally of logic and feeling: Beethoven, Bach. Thus, long before Siegfried Othmer stopped me just as I was getting on the school bus to go home, and asked me if I would be his date for the prom, and I said no, but only because—I was too stupid, and too groggy, to tell him this—I had been up all night the night before reading or studying or writing or doing something, drawing a time line that showed the different geological eras or working on my history of the world, something like that, I had promised myself to another life. I had come into the world pinned, pledged, and preoccupied. Preoccupied by a revelation I felt had been vouchsafed me and by a corollary recognition that my task was to help others see what had been revealed to me. I was born a lover and evangelist. Like all disciples, I did not feel driven; I felt called.

I used to think I was special, even weird, in this regard, but now I suspect many, if not most, writers feel the same way. Writers' art is by the nature of its medium an art that both shows and tells, creates and seeks to understand. When I was young, I thought of myself as having been given a "mission"—that is the word I used, but only silently, to myself, because it would have been presumptuous, if not just plain foolhardy, to say it aloud.

Some kids believe they must have been stolen from their real parents and will someday be restored to their rightful inheritance, acknowledged at last as special. Maybe my mission was nothing more than a fantasy. There wasn't a lot of evidence that I would ever fulfill it. I wasn't, at least not often, one of those children who write stories at the age of eight or publish sonnets at twelve, and for years I simply listened to music, read, daydreamed, and tried to copy Kim Novak's haircut.

We'd left Baton Rouge when I was four, spending the summer on a lake outside Toronto, where my younger sister and I took turns rolling sideways in the washtub and we heard loons and had leeches pulled off of us and our big brother shot up and turned golden brown and dived off a cliff. In the fall we joined our father in Ithaca, New York, moving into the tenement apartment that would be our home for five years. Our parents were desperately busy, but my mother still found time to sew sequins onto my sister's and my cardboard cut-out crowns for our Halloween costumes. One year my mother dressed me as a "medieval lady," but the judges—she said—were looking the other way when I walked by. She made a stubborn point about not forgiving those judges in the grandstand, though the point quickly became a joke. She was not interested in what we now call "parenting"—I don't believe it ever occurred to her that children might require "raising"; she simply assumed that we were smart enough to figure things out on our own and, besides, needed us to do that, because she was profoundly dedicated to music and wanted to play the violin as well as possible and side by side with our father—but she was young and lively and full of fun, at least until post-war poverty in a cold, gray town populated by humorless Yankees wore her down. Finally my parents were able to escape what to them had proved a depressing, exhausting, bare-bones existence. They escaped to Richmond, Virginia.

All that time, nobody bothered me much. A little: there were a couple of brouhahas involving conflicts with parents about vocational goals. First, I announced I was quitting the piano in order to become a writer. I was twelve. My mother said that she would rather kill me than have me turn out like my brother, a beatnik. I was standing in the doorway of my bedroom and my mother and father were facing me from the hallway. My mother screamed, "I'm not going to have another Mike in this house!" and then she ran to the kitchen to get the butcher knife. She was gone and then she was back in the hall, at the bedroom, knife upraised. She didn't look crazed; she just looked like she wanted to get the hell rid of me. She brought the knife down toward me, and my father grabbed her by the arms and forced her to drop it. It clattered on the floor and he picked it up and returned it to the kitchen.

Next I wrote a long poem in rhyming quatrains. (It was Shakespeare who had caused me to do this; I was in love with the singing line, the felt idea, a rampaging world controlled by structure, the fantastic as a mirror of reality.) The teacher gave my poem a C. When she handed it back to me, I cried in spite of trying hard not to, but my grade stayed a C. She said she was grading "in relation to what you are capable of." Yet I had done the best I could do—pages and pages of quatrains titled "The Winter's Tale." I knew I couldn't write any better than that.

The following year I submitted a story to my high-school literary magazine; it was a story about a man, a failed writer, who was thinking of killing himself, quite likely with a butcher knife. As he walked along the street, deep in despair, he passed a conservatory. From one of the windows came the sounds of a pianist practicing the *Waldstein* Sonata. Hearing this music, beautiful beyond words, the man resolved to live. The editors of the literary magazine declined to publish my story, on the grounds that it was too depressing.

I told my guidance counselor, who asked me what my vocational goals were, that I was interested in writing, science, and drama. "Well," she said, "why don't you write science fiction shows for television?"

In high school, when I was writing, late at night, my attic room cool at last briefly before dawn, I was possibly the happiest person on earth. I copied the final paragraph of *Moby-Dick* into a spiral notebook, feeling the long line of the words play itself out under my hands like the line attached to a harpoon. I pored over the battle scenes in *War and Peace*, reckoning them essential to the music of the whole.

This was the first room I had to myself, and it was magical. There was a wooden seat under the dormer window. My brother did some complicated wiring that allowed me to turn the downstairs dining-room radio on and off from upstairs, so I could listen to the all-night classical station; I could also stack records on the downstairs player and listen to them on a speaker he'd put in my room. I had a closet with a small dresser and mirror at one end and no door, so I could primp in my babydoll (that meant short and filmy, very Tennessee Williams) pajamas while working on that Kim Novak hair style. My parents' room was in the attic at the other end, and they'd built in some privacy for themselves by putting in floor-to-ceiling bookshelves that formed a hallway from the stairs to my room. They did much of the carpentry and painting, thrilled to own a house at last. It was a tiny white stucco house, but when I was at my end of the attic, I might as well have been alone on an island.

My mother tried to make peace with me. She asked to see some of my poetry. That was when I showed her a poem in which I used the word *nipple*. She had a mock heart attack. None of us knew it was "mock," of course—not even she did—and when the doctor came to his house, black bag in hand, I thought I had killed my mother with my shameless poem.

"You must be careful," she said to me, on another occasion, "not to have more success than your big brother. He decided to be a writer first. And he's a boy."

My father took some of my work to one of his colleagues at Richmond Professional Institute. The colleague wrote me a letter in which he said I had a "flare" [*sic*] for words but that girls grew out of this kind of thing.

Even though I hadn't yet grown out of my wish to write, I had to quit writing for the foreseeable future in order to study science and mathematics. This was another of the many schemes that were launched on behalf of my future: I would be a pianist, a housewife, an actress, a secretary, a scientist. An Indian chief, a candle maker. Science was now in the ascendence, and at seventeen I was transferring to the New Mexico Institute of Science and Technology for my sophomore year. (I was never allowed to apply to any of the undergraduate schools I wanted to attend; I suspect my mother was unconsciously reenacting *her* mother's refusal to let her go to her college of choice—where, they worried, she might follow in her sister's flapper footsteps. Around we go.) I made a note to myself about my academic obligation. "For the next several years," I wrote, "I must not write." But when I was kicked out of college for the second time and no college anywhere would enroll me, I wrote a novella, to show everyone I was serious about writing. It was called "The Silver Crow."

Luckily, a dean whose own daughter had been kicked out of school was fond of me because I reminded him of her, and he took me under his wing and got me reinstated. Back in school, I wrote an allegory about a man named Dev.

In my last summer of college—I was making up missed requirements—I took on a non-credit course that a sociology professor and I had devised. We just sat down together and made it up, and didn't even ask whether it could be for credit. We called this course "Creative Symbolism," and we read Freud, Durkheim, Benjamin Whorf, Cassirer, and on and on. Every day we'd meet in the campus soda shop for three, four, five hours at a time; reading for the course kept me up until three, four, or five in the morning. One day near the end of summer I worked up the courage to show him my allegory. For four hours, he told me how I had no talent for writing and should stick with analytic studies. He was diligent and kindly and concerned about me and had, after all, given his entire summer to me, and he tried to couch his criticism in gentle terms. When he was finished, I said thank you and left the table. At the top of the high staircase, I fainted. When I came to, the sociology professor and the school nurse were bending over me. "Is it that time of month, dear?" asked the nurse, in a whisper that the sociology professor was not supposed to hear but certainly did.

And this was how it went, for quite a long time. It would be nice to be able to say that I persevered, but sometimes I think the opposite is truer: I quit. I quit again and again, the way a thoroughly addicted smoker will keep quitting.

I quit writing when I got married. I quit again when I got divorced. Every day I would tell myself that I had no business writing, it was not what I deserved to be doing; this was indeed a little lecture I honed and delivered to myself in the morning before going to work—out loud. Writing was never anything I could just say no to. I had better luck quitting smoking—I haven't smoked since the second draft of my first novel.

When I write, I am still in my attic room. I am not worried about whether I will have too much success or too little. It does not matter if no one approves of what I am doing. It does not even matter if my mother, reading it, would want to kill herself. I was shameless then, and I am shameless now—the way addicts are. My mother never stood a chance (and eventually, she gave in and even supported my habit).

Writing is a state of being in which the hope of beauty and the quest for truth combine, like a mirage, like a dream of natural power, but the place you are trying to get to can never be gotten to because it is a place that, like great music, is beyond words. Shakespeare, Melville, and Tolstoy are like directions on a map, but not even they are the place itself, which, as Socrates suggested, is where your soul first resided and where you have so inarticulately longed to return ever since you unwittingly left it. It is a place of pure harmony. The thought of reaching it will keep you alive, though also entranced. It will fill you with a desire to write and write and write—stories like sonatas, novels like symphonies, poems like string quartets, the words spilling out of the window into the street for any despairing passerby to hear and be saved by. If your work does not do this, if no one is rescued, the impulse is still there. This is the intention: to create art that is irresistible, art that possesses the power to make us human beings—we paradoxical beings who are born haunted by our own skepticism—*want* to live. (And so it did matter about my mother, whether she wanted to kill herself or live—but I had to write, whether she resisted my work or not. Whether she had a real heart attack or only a mock one.)

Nonetheless, at my mother's suggestion I took typing in summer school and on my own elected to spend the savings from my first summer job, at sixteen, on private tutelage in algebra. So maybe she wasn't trying to rule my future; maybe, as she said, she was only trying to keep up with my exuberantly inclusive interests. "One day you want to be a chemist," she said. "The next day you want to be a drummer." Everybody knew that if I was going to write I had to be trained to do something else, because writers don't earn any money. I can't imagine how I got it into my head that drummers did.

I was twenty when I entered the University of Virginia as a graduate student in philosophy. There I met Henry Taylor, a sophomore, and R.H.W. (Richard) Dillard, a graduate student, both in the English department and both determined to be writers. Henry invited me to a small "bootleg" seminar, run by Fred Bornhauser, a professor of literature, which was, in effect, a non-credit poetry workshop. We met at night in a classroom in Cabell Hall. The next fall, George Garrett, young, acclaimed, energetic—and prolific, various, and published—and generous, empathetic, and prankish—arrived to teach an official writing class, the first such class at the University of Virginia—and quickly became the charismatic center and guiding light of our literary activities.

Although I grew up in the South and at a time when women were not generally granted credibility as artists—or as doctors or scientists or scholars or corporate executives—I was incredibly blessed in my literary friendships. George, Henry, and Richard took my ambition seriously; and if any one of them ever questioned it, he didn't let me know. At the time I took for granted that they were my good friends and writing buddies; now I look back and think how amazingly fortunate I was to find them. If there was a sexist bone in any one of their bodies I never knew it. The women's movement hadn't started, yet here and there were men who never thought to delimit a young woman's world but, on the contrary, helped to open the world to her. In her essay for the *Contemporary Authors* Autobiography Series, Rita Dove wrote that when she arrived in Charlottesville in 1989 to teach at the University of Virginia she found it "[h]ard to imagine that a mere twenty-five to thirty years ago this university was a fortress of racism and male chauvinism!" It had been, but there were those within who were working, deliberately or not, self-consciously or not, to open the gates, let down the drawbridge. Every revolution is heralded quietly, by individuals who choose to think or act in a new way.

I needed to cross over that bridge, walk into the world. Toward that end, I returned to Richmond to look for work. I worked three jobs at once, a day job, a night job, and a weekend job, to save money for a trip to Europe (I guess it took that many jobs because women earned so little; typing addresses on envelopes, we were paid by the envelope). Then I boarded a freighter to Amsterdam.

People frequently say that when they look back over their lives they can hardly recognize their earlier selves. Who was the young woman who, excessively shy though she was, nevertheless found herself in the Hotel Metropol in Moscow, in January 1965, communicating in makeshift sign language with the young Latvian composer Imants Kalniņš, already well known in the Soviet Union both for his music and his independence? (The KGB, I would learn, was busily asking this same question. They asked it while they sat in their white Volvo, watching us from their parking place behind the trees at the edge of the cemetery outside Riga, at midnight, when we said good-bye.) I have no trouble recognizing her as myself. Someone else might—I certainly no longer look like that young woman. But something in her eyes, the mere fact that she is in Moscow and is having a conversation with a composer whose language she doesn't know, seems, *feels*, true to form. I was always shy; I was always cautious; and I was always too curious about the world to stay home.

The University of North Carolina at Greensboro was the perfect place, and it was where I went after I returned from Europe. It was sleepy, out of the mainstream; the teachers were not in the celebrity game, and Fred Chappell, Robert Watson,

Allen Tate, Guy Owen, Peter Taylor, and Randall Jarrell conveyed their love of the highest standards. Visiting writers included Eudora Welty and Carolyn Kizer.

At the University of Virginia I had been too scared to submit my work to the usual competitions—the Academy of American Poets contests, for example (how could I survive the shame of an Honorable Mention?); now, when our work was to be discussed by a festival of visiting writers, I hid out in an empty classroom. I *wanted* to hear Stanley Kunitz and X. J. Kennedy, poets I admired tremendously, discuss our apprentice poems, but, again, what if what they had to say was defeating? And earlier, as soon as Stanley Kunitz arrived on campus and was introduced to a few of us students, in somebody's living room, he had begun to exclaim about his protegée, Louise Glück. I didn't know how he was going to find room in his attention span for another young poet. And if X. J. Kennedy didn't like my poems I was going to have to drown myself.

All this exquisite agony was no doubt silliness, a waste of time and energy, not to mention the waste of good contacts (I knew my teachers were trying to help me meet writers—they tried to help all the students meet writers), but perhaps it had its uses, too. It allowed me the solitude to read as unstoppingly as I always had, but having previously focused on philosophers, playwrights, and classical literature in translation, I felt especially eager to shore up the gaps created by not having taken literature classes in college. I bought survey texts for American and British literature and read them through; I collected syllabi and worked my way through them; and of course, I wandered the aisles of UNC-G's Jackson Library, sitting on the floor whenever I found a book that called to me to open it.

My lack of social skills gave me leeway to follow my own literary instincts, which I did, writing a long sequential poem, "Benjamin John," that told the story of a man's life—Mr. John was an imagined economics professor—through lyrical or dramatic moments.

A few weeks ago, my old classmate William Pitt (Bill) Root reminded me that he and I met with Allen Tate at a Greensboro diner to discuss our work. Mr. Tate decided to begin with me. "Tell me," he began, "why a woman who looks like you would want to write from a male point of view?" Bill said we were both stunned; he assured me that I recovered from my surprise immediately and answered Mr. Tate clearly and "firmly." I hope so. But the women's movement *still* hadn't started, and a girl's responses to male chauvinism could be hit or miss. (Despite this incident, Tate was an exacting and inspiring teacher.)

Besides, the girl I was wanted to be loved as much as she wanted to be published. Having been told by Soviet authorities that I would not be permitted to marry Imants, and having mourned the loss of him for nearly two years, I fell in love with and married Jonathan Silver, a sculptor, who had arrived at UNC-G in the capacity of visiting art historian.

That fall marked the publication of *The Girl in the Black Raincoat*, an anthology of fiction and poetry edited by George Garrett and inspired by my black raincoat. After I'd moved from Charlottesville back to Richmond, Henry wrote a story for George's class about "the girl in the black raincoat." When he read it to the class, many of the students were disturbed, thinking it was wrong of him, somehow immoral, to have written about someone they knew, someone who was not completely made up. To help them understand the complex relationship between reality and fiction, George directed the whole class to write stories about a girl in a black raincoat. But—why stop there? he wondered, and conceived the anthology. Contributors included Annie Dillard, Henry Taylor, Leslie Fiedler, Mary Lee Settle, Carolyn Kizer, others. Donald Justice and Mark Strand produced a co-authored poem. All the authors had all had described to them—or some of them knew—a girl who used to wear a black raincoat even on sunny days. (I meant merely to use it as a sweater; my mother had bought it for me in downtown Richmond.)

It was the publication parties thrown for *The Girl in the Black Raincoat*, at Hollins College and in Charlottesville, that persuaded me I ought to be married: Everyone else—it seemed to me—was; everyone else had a real life as a real person and not just as a fantasy; everyone else knew enough not to go to a publication party without a poem stuck in her coat pocket. It hadn't even occurred to me that we would be giving readings! I knew Jonathan would ask me to marry him if I let him know I was available for marriage; he did, and I said yes.

(If I'd been smarter I might have known that I had also met the man I should have—and now have—married, but I wouldn't find this out for another three decades. More about him later.)

My mother liked Jonathan. She and my father picked us up at the bus station the weekend we went to Richmond for a blood test. Jonathan and I got in the back seat. "Would you like a Life Saver?" my mother asked him, turning around to offer him the opened roll. "Too late," he said, and she was his.

Or would have been, if he had not been so determined to go at everything as if it were an obstacle. My mother gave me a handful of recipes, taught me how to make a white sauce, cautioned me that men's egos need bolstering. She and my father did their best to help us out, but Jonathan was suspicious of every gesture, every offer. It's no wonder: his own father asked him what it would cost to convince me I should break off the engagement ("go away" was how he put it, or "get lost"), informed him he was disowned, and forbade Jonathan's mother to see her son, a commandment she broke once or twice but not comfortably. They did not come to the wedding in Richmond.

Which may have been just as well.

In the end, Jonathan decided he did not want children. Before I accepted his proposal I had asked him if he did, and he said yes, but now he did not. Now he wanted a divorce, and though I had at first been the one less in love, that had changed while we were together; and it took me years, after the divorce, to recover a sense of self. I stayed in New York to do this, working in children's books, teaching at a private school for emotionally disturbed kids, and tutoring a teenager who had cerebral palsy.

I was starting a new job on Monday. I had been asked, on the basis of some freelance copy editing I had done, to write a teacher's guide to Jewish morality tales. I spent the weekend smoking hash with a male friend. On Monday morning, I called my new boss to tell him I would not be coming in after all because I was thinking of killing myself and would therefore probably not be available for employment. "Let's have lunch first," he said. At lunch, he suggested that I write down what had happened. I no longer believed I could write a story and so I wrote him a long letter, even though he had been my boss for only a couple of days. He showed the letter to the writer Abraham Rothberg, who nudged, coaxed, challenged, and persuaded me to make a story of it. He plastered the margins with X's, each indicating a scene in want of development, and paid no attention at all to my reluctance. *Commentary* published the story, and when my dry cleaner and his wife recognized my name, as they told me when I handed him the ticket for the clothes I had dropped off, I felt famous and started writing again. Abe became a dear friend, one who has never pulled any punches, always telling me frankly what he liked and didn't like about my work. He is a distinguished journalist and novelist, with particular expertise in the history of World War II. We have kept up a correspondence for years now; I save his letters.

Even so, it was a difficult time. Young women writers were not usually taken seriously, and there was not the same career ladder for writers, male or female, then that there is now. I wasn't close friends with established writers or magazine editors; I earned a pittance (and soon I had a day job, a night job, a weekend job); every morning I delivered my you-are-not-a-writer lecture to myself with my first cup of coffee, hoping I could teach myself to want less, to settle for what I had.

One day Con Edison turned off my electricity because a previous, extremely previous, tenant had not paid his bill. The representative on the telephone refused to believe that I was not that tenant. I said I had a sick child. Whether she believed me or not, the representative was required by law to turn the electricity back on after that. I was ashamed of myself, but pleased, too, and

I figured that if I could holler at Con Ed and get them to do what I wanted, I had learned to be a New Yorker and my sense of self was back in working order. I started work on my first novel, *Sick and Full of Burning*, and by the time I left New York City, passing up a raise and promotion and leave time to move back, broke, to Richmond, because I didn't think I could maintain the faith in New York, I had a rough draft.

Sick and Full of Burning recounts the adventures of a medical student, Mary (Tennessee) Settleworth, living in New York City, who earns her tuition by working as a live-in tutor to a handicapped teenager. The book poses this question: Am I my sister's keeper, even if that entails martyrdom? My protagonist answers the question with a *no* and yet, contrarily, acts out the answer *yes*, risking her life for her student's. This is how I put it to a newspaper interviewer: "The fire is the apocalypse. It is that extreme event at the point of which one comes to terms with whether or not one wants to live. Tennessee is unclear about her affection for life and she takes this question right down to the wire, which in this instance is the fire." It is in the consideration of questions that seem to permit, or even require, absolute and contradictory answers that I find the real subjects of my novels. Invited by *Library Journal* to say something about my first novel in 1974, I explained, "I took as my starting point Deuteronomy 30:19, '...I have set before you life and death...therefore choose life...,' surely the wildest non sequitur in Western civilization, and set out to see what steps might be supplied that would establish a logical progression from the possibility of suicide, real or moral, to the injunction to reject it as an alternative. That's why the structure of the book is a spiral, like one of those slinky coils which walk down stairs to the delight of children, and why the book circles its own center on successive levels before it reaches the bottom." I wanted what appeared to be a comedy about three women to turn itself inside out, like a Moebius strip, halfway through, revealing its tragic dimension.

While I was working on *Sick and Full of Burning* in Richmond, my mother decided to write a book about moving to England—as she and my father planned to do in retirement—and as it happened, my brother joined us to work on a nonfiction manuscript that would become *On High Steel*, about life as an ironworker. All three books were published in 1974—probably the first time three first books in one family appeared in one year. My mother was awarded a medal from the English-speaking Union. *Kirkus Reviews* called *Sick and Full of Burning* "a just about perfect first novel—bright, sassy, sad and with talent, well, to burn." *The Chicago Tribune Book World* exclaimed, "A flawless first novel? You gotta be kidding! No kidding." *People* magazine singled me out for a "Lookout" article in July of 1974. Mass paperback rights sold to Ballantine Books. In short, the successes of my mother's and my books were satisfying, no matter how modest. My brother's success was greater: NBC featured his book in five five-minute segments on the national *Evening News* one week. We were happy campers. My father took to saying he was going to write a book called *The Old Man and the C Scale*. None of us had an inkling about how rough things were going to turn. Nor did I yet care—I thought I would write my books, get them published, and continue to receive astonishing praise from serious and smart reviewers.

I had always thought of myself as a poet first and foremost, but I had not been able to publish much poetry after leaving UNC-G (even though I had published a fair amount of it while I was a student, including "Benjamin John" in *The Carolina Quarterly*, and three of my poems had been set by my father and performed in concert). It wasn't until later that I realized that my interest in form, meter, and rhyme was out of sync with the poetry of that period. (There was also the question whether my poems deserved to be published.) When a small press in North Carolina called to ask me about my manuscript—Fred Chappell had referred the press to me; as I said, I would have been *lost* without my friends—I gladly seized the opportunity. *Lovers and*

Agnostics, my first collection of poems, which included "Benjamin John," appeared in 1975.

At that point I figured I had forfeited five years to being married and then to being divorced, and I didn't want to lose more time. I tried to sort out what books, poetry and prose, I wanted to write. (Perhaps I should have thought instead about the business of becoming a writer—sales, agents, networking for freelance pieces—but I concentrated on the books themselves— my subjects, characters, imagery, the forms and structures.) I visualized a bookshelf holding the books I wished to write. This time I say "visualized" because it *was* something like a vision, although making out the titles on the spines, or even just knowing which volume was poetry and which fiction, occupied my evenings for some weeks. I have never been rigid about what I would write, but a number of my books derive from that period of thinking about how I would fill the shelf. I also revised the lecture I delivered to myself daily from "You are not a writer" to "If you don't write your books, no one else will."

It was a gratification to see *Lovers and Agnostics* published. After all, in my mind I was a poet first, even if the first *book* I'd published was a novel. I turned to my poems-in-progress, which were already adding up. The publication of my second collection, *Relativity: A Point of View,* in 1977 marked the beginning of my very happy relationship with Louisiana State University Press, a relationship that has been, for me, both sustaining and guiding.

The final poem in *Relativity,* "A Bird's-eye View of Einstein," is an examination of the idea of the Trinity from a woman's point of view. In blank verse, the poem's three sections pursue various trinities: Son, Ghost, Father; husband, brother, father; Freud's three universal taboos of cannibalism, incest, murder; the three major prophets of the Old Testament (each presented in a "sermon"), Jeremiah, Ezekiel, Isaiah; the ideas of covenant, honesty, judgment; the tree of good and evil, the tree of community, the tree of faith in Revelation; future, past, present; sex, politics, creative knowledge; city, ocean, desert; Richmond, Ithaca, Baton Rouge; taste, light, sound. But because the poem is using the idea of relativity to look at the idea of trinity, it is not a simple scheme of threes: After a prologue introduces "the point of view," a bird's-eye point of view, which seems to be outside the trinities, the body of the poem rings changes on the point of view, finally returning to a bird's point of view, only now it is a different bird, or the bird itself seen from a different point of view; the bird is *time that flies*: "Time/ Sings in the tree." Thus the Trinity, which is three-in-one, is one and one and one—and one.

Some reviewers have found the imagery overwhelming—overwrought, they sometimes say—not recognizing that much of it comes from the Book of Revelation and the three major prophets of the Old Testament—Isaiah, Ezekiel, and Jeremiah, nor that the tripartite structure of the poem is built on a number of levels, all of them sliced through by a point-of-view that shifts. I might wonder if what I thought I'd put into the poem had really got into the poem were it not that Fred Chappell, having already sent me a short, nice note about the book upon publication, wrote me again three months later, single-spaced, front and back, several pages, explaining with some excitement how my poem was put together. His analysis reflected precisely what I had thought I was doing.

Fred has since changed his mind about the poem, finding it ambitious but ultimately a failure. That he now thinks this doesn't bother me, because it's also now what I think. At the heart of the poem was a secret—a secret I was trying, in the poem, to tell—but which I was afraid to tell. Moreover, as shocking as I thought that secret would be if revealed, I was also hiding *from myself* my own deepest feeling, a humiliating feeling, the feeling of rejection. I believed this feeling of rejection was eternal, which is why the poem hints at the idea of eternal recurrence. There was never going to be any relief from this feeling.

A couple of years ago, Fred asked me who I think of as my audience. "You," I said. He seemed surprised. "I would have thought it was your parents," he said. My parents are sometimes my subjects—with their permission, I might add—but not my audience, even emotionally. The audience I think of myself as writing for is made up of readers I admire, whose serious regard and respect I want to earn. Some are writers, some not. Of course I was pleased whenever my parents responded positively to something I wrote. But if I had been writing for that positive response, I would not only not have written certain works— including anything with the word "nipple" in it—I would not have written at all after the age of twelve. This doesn't seem a problem to me; my parents did not play their violins for their parents' applause. They didn't play for their children's applause, either. Neither my parents nor I used an art form for purposes of rebellion. They made music because music was what each of them was born to make. I write because I have to.

In a *credo* on the jacket flap of *Relativity*, I gave my view of what I was up to:

> I'm concerned with the shape of ideas in time: the dynamic configuration a moral dilemma makes, cutting through a novel like a river through rock; the way a philosophical statement bounces against the walls of a poem, like an echo in a canyon. A writer, poet or novelist, wants to create a contained, complete landscape in which time flows freely and naturally. The *poems* are where I live. It's in poetry that thought and time most musically counterpoint each other, and I like a world in which the elements sing.

Imants Kalniņš would sometimes call me up from Moscow or Riga. In the summer of 1975, right after the Helsinki Accords were signed, I went back to Riga, and we tried again to get married. This time the KGB threatened us, made anonymous phone calls in the middle of the night, took photographs. After I left—my visa had expired—they frequently intercepted our mail, and we had to smuggle letters back and forth.

I no longer had a home base in the States. My parents had moved to England for their retirement—they wanted to listen to music, and they wanted to be near my sister, a solo flutist specializing in contemporary music and professor at London School of Music and Trinity School of Music—so I joined them there, thinking I'd soon be allowed back in to the Soviet Union. I didn't know that I would not see Imants again until 1988, when he was invited to the States to attend the premiere of his fifth symphony.... I was to spend the next two years in England, studying Latvian with a BBC translator, and writing, among other things, my second novel, a modern-day restoration comedy about marriage and music. (I made the heroine a flutist.)

In a paperback of George Crabbe's poetry I'd found an epigraph that seemed to fit the young married couple I was writing about. I happened to mail the epigraph to my brother, who wrote back suggesting that two words in it, "Augusta played," would make a good title. Suddenly the book took off. I had a great time writing this book—my "golden" book, as I thought of it, for Augusta was herself a golden beauty, and her flute with its gold mouthpiece was a metaphor for how I wanted my prose to sing.

Augusta Played addresses the question I saw as being the logical next stop among the fiction entries on my bookshelf: Assuming that one *has* chosen to live, are one's other choices determined or free? Again, it seemed that this was a question to which both answers, contradictory though they are, could be supported. This time I supplied the contradictory answers by opposing two main characters, a husband and wife, the one representing a deterministic world view, the other free will. The wife, Augusta, is a flutist studying at Juilliard; her husband, Norman, is the first known "cultural musicologist," a field he has invented for himself, and a doctoral candidate at Columbia University. The two characters are presented with equal sympathy, as are a large cast of minor characters encompassing, among others, a stripper, a judge, an orchestra conductor, a blackmailer, two little boys (one of whom talks like Aldo Ray), and a synthesizer. How could I not have had a great time?

But in the real, unfictional world, I was a citizen of one country, living in a second country, seeking permission to live in a third country, and I was also broke. When one day I got a call from the University of Wisconsin at Madison asking me if I'd like to come be a visiting lecturer for a year, I said yes.

At UW-Madison, I had a staggering load. Many professors do, in contrast to the popular notion of the professorial life. At least I had a novel in hand: *Augusta Played* was published in my second year at UW-Madison. It would be some time before I came out with another. Sans tweed jacket with leather elbow patches, sans pipe, sans evenings before the fire in the fireplace, glass of cognac in hand, with, in fact, approximately four thousand five hundred pages of student manuscript to read and mark up each semester, not counting work submitted by tutorial students, I wrote a long unpublished novel—but only by dint of giving up any hope of a personal life. Unfortunately, the novel, Paula, an examination of rage and frustration—that is, of what happens when one's choices conflict with another's—bore the marks of depression and exhaustion and is unpublishable as it stands. I like to think that somewhere in what became an incohesive, rambling mutter ("I will write no matter what," "I will write no matter what") a short, tight novel waits to be found, but I am reluctant to look for it, for fear it might not, after all, be there.

I put Paula away and began work on *In the Wink of an Eye*, which remains one of my favorite books. The question posed here was, Is revolution ever a just way of creating a just state? The novel is a political cartoon. The contradiction suggested by the question (*yes* and *no*) is sustained via a *reductio ad absurdum* in which a small revolution that begins in the infamous Green Hell of the Santa Cruz State in Bolivia succeeds beyond its most extravagant dreams—succeeds, that is to say, *as* its most extravagant dreams, spreading first to other parts of the world and then *beyond* the world, into outer space and the realm of the imagination, for it is a part of my political program, as I say in the book, that "it is the inalienable right of the imagination to rejoice in itself."

To cover the ground I needed to cover—several continents and then no ground at all!—I converted the idea of an omniscient "I" into "God's eye." The action could take place wherever God's eye happened to glance in a given chapter. A further motive behind this novel was Northrop Frye's caveat against conjoining romance and satire; had I not already intended to write the book,

Frye's rule alone would probably have caused me to think of it. From the beginning I have enjoyed taking as challenges any advice about or analysis of writing that has seemed to me to limit, politically or aesthetically, the domain of the creative spirit.

I wish that *Wink* might have found more readers or at least had a chance to look for them, but it was an orphan book. *Sick and Full of Burning* had also been an orphan book, as was, in a two-book contract, *The Lost Traveller's Dream*, meaning the editor who had accepted it was gone from the publishing house before the book was published. *Augusta Played* wound up with a different house—Houghton Mifflin. I had no continuity with a house or editor and none of the books received much promotion. *Wink* and *Traveller* were given a sandwich and an apple and abandoned by the side of the road. So Louisiana State University Press's recent reissue of *Wink* as a Voices of the South paperback has been a surprise that feels to me like a gift.

The Lost Traveller's Dream continued the exploration of the theme of the imagination that I had begun in *In the Wink of an Eye*, but in a non-comic mode. With an epigraph taken from the poem by William Blake in which he says (speaking to Satan), "Every Harlot was a Virgin once,/ Nor can'st thou ever change Kate into Nan," the book proceeds to change Kate into Nan. Kate, who is the narrator of the three stories of the first part, is the editor and writer who has created Lindy, the photographer and poet of the second part. Only in the third and final section do we learn that Kate was herself a created character, devised by Nan who reveals her working method in a series of stories in which Kate is one among many characters. In other words, Lindy has represented a dead-end of self-involvement that leads only to a loss of faith—embodied as a friend—while Nan turns the creative attention outward to embrace the world in which she lives. This is, ultimately, a work that argues process is product, and imagination, reality. "We were ourselves only part of a larger story," the book concludes, having brought the three narrators together in an editorial *we*, "whose ending we could not know, a dénouement that would find us whether or not we could find it...."

The conclusion, lost to us in mystery, reveals itself in the act of self-knowledge, God's mind learning its own power."

At about this time I came across an article by David R. Slavitt and wrote to him about it. I had met David years before, at the *Girl in the Black Raincoat* party at Charlottesville, but we didn't know each other. He answered my letter, and out of that grew a fine friendship with another tremendously smart and learned man. It was David who defined George Garrett, Fred Chappell, R. H. W. Dillard, Brendan Galvin, Henry Taylor, himself, and me as "pleiades" in an anthology by that title.

I knew I was going to have trouble finding a publisher for another novel, and one Saturday night, as I worked on a story titled "War and Peace," I realized that by excerpting a few pages from a novella I had thrown aside a few years earlier, and two pages from an unpublished piece of ten years earlier, and adding stories about this, this, and that, I would have a group of stories that I would be able to publish individually, in magazines and journals, and that could also be put together to form a book-length narrative.

My Life and Dr. Joyce Brothers was billed by the publisher as a novel in stories. The overarching narrative does justify, I believe, the term *novel in stories*—a description I would have been happy to apply to *The Lost Traveller's Dream*—but eventually this book is to be seen as Book One of a story cycle; my next published fiction, *The Society of Friends* (1999), is Book Two; and there will be a third book. I don't think uncommercial writers are often able to publish long works of fiction, especially when the books have been previously published by different houses, but that is my dream: to see the three in one volume, so that the shape of the whole will be clear.

My Life and Dr. Joyce Brothers was my first published fiction to refer to Madison, Wisconsin. In these stories about a woman, Nina Bryant, moving away from her own family and creating for herself a nontraditional family of friends, Madison becomes the nexus of comment about contemporary American society. *The*

Society of Friends expands the fictional territory to the lives of some of Nina's neighbors. Among them are a high-school Latin teacher, a nurse, a commodities broker, a gallery owner, a medical librarian, a performance artist. They are decent people trying to live decent lives.

Eleven years elapsed between my second and third poetry collections. This was not because I was not writing poems or not submitting a poetry manuscript to publishers. *Natural Theology* was rescued by Henry Taylor, who looked at the manuscript when he was in Madison to give a reading and advised me to shorten it and switch the opening poems to later in the book. I asked him why they shouldn't stay at the beginning. "Because they are too peculiar," Henry said. "Nobody will know how to read them."

Writers who believe in the language must also believe in one another. I doubt that I would ever have succeeded in publishing anything, and I know I would not have published everything I have published, without the help and encouragement of such good friends. From them, I have learned to extend a similar hand wherever I can.

Natural Theology provided the occasion for the Fellowship of Southern Writers Poetry Award, the Hanes Poetry Prize, though the prize is awarded for a body of work rather than a single book. The presentation, in Chattanooga, was one of the most exciting events of my professional life. I, and the winners of other prizes, stood on a stage in front of an audience of 1,500, many of whom were members of the literary establishment. I thought I would be speechless with stage fright, but as soon as I gripped the podium and looked out into the auditorium, I felt right at home up there. Probably a writer should not be moved by appeals to her vanity, but I was, I admit I was, and in the photographs taken after the ceremony, I couldn't stop smiling.

The title of my fourth book of poems, *God's Loud Hand*, comes from one of the poems, "Song for the Second Creation," in which "love" is "the sung word flung into the world by God's loud hand." The "sung word" referred to is Christ; the "loud hand" refers to the sound of one hand clapping, as in the well-known zen koan. After the book appeared, some readers assumed that I am a devout Christian. I'm not.

Death and Transfiguration, which arose out of a time of loss—the illnesses and deaths of my parents, my ex-husband, and others—closes with a long poem titled "Requiem," wherein I endeavor to deal directly and systematically with the question posed by Theodor Adorno—can art be made, in good conscience, after the horror of the Holocaust? The poem is an argument and adheres to its line(s) of thought, deriving in conclusion a crucial distinction between experience, which is personal and subjective, and memory, which can be articulated and shared. At the same time, it sweeps up and holds together the losses tallied in the book's first, and only other, section.

I agree with W. H. Auden that the minor artist is the one who cleaves to a competency instead of risking failure; a necessary condition, whether sufficient or not, for the artist aspiring to major achievement is that she avoid self-parody or a mannerist version of herself, and that means she has to keep pushing in unfamiliar directions, tackling the new. Perhaps, therefore, it is *better* not to be noticed, since notice tends to make writers hunger for more of it, which they are apt to go after by repeating whatever has brought them notice.

Rising Venus, which came out in 2002, looks at the experience of being female. My collection *Hazard and Prospect: New and Selected Poems* was published in 2007. A book-length sonnet sequence about philosophy is slated for 2009.

Accepting that I was going to be a writer whether or no, my mother became as supportive and helpful as any daughter could hope. She read reams of work-in-progress; responded to my compulsively anxious queries about whether to use this word or that, this punctuation or that; told me to keep going when I imagined I should quit; and typed the entire handwritten draft of *The Exiled Heart*.

She typed it on her old manual, with the keys that had to be hammered half a mile down. I left the draft pages on the dining room table when I went to bed, and when I got up, I found them side by side with the typed pages. I wrote the first draft while I was still living in England, still trying to get a visa to return to Latvia in order to marry Imants. The book details that quest: the struggle of a man and a woman against arbitrary obstacles placed in their path by politicos and bureaucrats. It is a love story with a sad ending. It is also an autobiographical inquiry into meaning, making essayistic excursions into the kinds of things one thinks about in a situation like that: What is justice? Is forgiveness possible? What does the artist owe to art? And of course, What is love? As I explained in the opening chapter, "I didn't know, in 1965, where [the] train was taking me: to Moscow, I thought, but equally to my heart and my conscience. This book is a kind of log, a moral travelogue if you will, of a course that was set then and there, deep into heartland." The central question of the book is, What can love mean in a corrupt world? As has often been the case for me, there was a long lapse between the first writing and publication—fifteen or sixteen years, a revised draft every year or year and a half—and the Soviet Union fell six months after the book came out. A brief essay, "What Is Poetry? What Is Music?" collected in my book *History, Passion, Freedom, Death, and Hope: Prose about Poetry,* functions as a coda to *The Exiled Heart* telling the story of our meeting in 1997, when the Detroit Symphony Orchestra, with Maestro Neeme Järvi, offered the world premiere of the original version of Imants's Fourth Symphony, whose last movement is set to poems I had written for Imants. The Soviet authorities had insisted that the English text be omitted; now, post-Soviet tyranny, it had been returned to the music, and changes made in the score to accommodate the revision were also returned to the original. I included the poems in my first collection; the symphony has been made available on a BIS compact disc, played by the Singapore Symphony Orchestra.

(My book *Writing the World* includes other pieces about my time behind the Iron Curtain, along with essays on writing and the writer's life.)

I love when, writing, I lose track of myself, my self works free of the constraint of time. It's time that allows us to recognize ourselves as selves, and when we forget ourselves, we live, however briefly, outside time. We know eternity, if only for a moment.

In 1999 I retired from UW-Madison. Burke Davis III, a fiction writer, and I were married September 17, 2000, in the small farmhouse we bought in southside Virginia. I sometimes teach as a visitor: a semester at Hollins University, in Roanoke, was a wonderful reunion with my good old friend Richard Dillard, and several terms at the University of Alabama in Huntsville, where I served as the Humanities Center's Visiting Eminent Scholar, have brought me new friendships and new experiences, both of which I treasure. In fact, teaching at UAH was one of the great pleasures of my life. I have recently taught at Colgate and Mercer universities and cherish my time in both places.

Our small farm is, of course, another pleasure. It is my husband who deserves all the credit here—he makes our country life possible, by being good at all the things I haven't a clue how to do. We have forty-four acres, including an orchard, woods, a pond, and a vegetable garden. It's because of Burke that I can look out my window (the glass is from 1874) at the small rain falling on loblolly pines. Intermittently the pianissimo mizzle strengthens to a hard shower loud on the tin roof.

But Burke is the center of my life.

I wish my parents could have known Burke, and that I am married to him. "You're so pretty," my mother said, after my father had died (I was forty-six, but she was my *mother*); "I wish you'd get a job somewhere else, find a good man, and get married." By then, we both knew I wasn't going to be a literary celebrity, that no grandstand judge was ever going to look my way, and although she didn't want me to quit writing, she did want me to have a happier life. If she were here, I could tell her that I do.

Part of what makes my life happy is my knowledge that I've written at least some of the books I planned to write (I hope to write all the books on my mental bookshelf). It's impossible not to wish that Burke and I had rediscovered each other earlier; maybe I could have been married *and* had kids *and* written my books *and* earned a living, but maybe we wouldn't have been ready earlier. As it was, I think I made the right choice. I have had an enduring relationship with writing, with the dream of creating something lasting, something memorable, some poem or novel or story that would do what I think art should do— bring beauty and truth together in a way that will help others to know what the late Beethoven string quartets taught me; namely, that artists make meaning, and meaning is celebration, triumph, the most miraculous of miracles. Meaning is *logos*, and without it there never was a beginning, not to anything, not to us, not to the greatest story ever told and not even to the least.

BIBLIOGRAPHY

AUTHORITY

Auden, W. H. "The Art of Poetry: No. 17." Interviewed by Michael Newman. New York: Paris Review 57 (1974): 20.

Byron, George Gordon Byron, Baron. "So, We'll Go No More A-Roving." The Works of Lord Byron: Letters and Journals. Edited by Rowland E. Prothero. 6 vols. London: John Murray, 1898.

Camus, Albert. The Rebel. Translated by Anthony Bower. New York: Knopf, 1954.

Eliot, T. S. The Sacred Wood: Essays on Poetry and Criticism. London: Methuen, 1920; New York: Knopf, 1930.

Frost, Robert. "The Figure a Poem Makes." Collected Poems of Robert Frost, 1939. Garden City, NY: H. Holt, 1939. Also, The Collected Prose of Robert Frost. Edited by Mark Richardson. Cambridge, MA: Belknap Press of Harvard University Press, 2007.

Jarrell, Randall. "The Age of Criticism." Poetry and the Age. New York: Knopf, 1953. Also, No Other Book: Selected Essays/Randall Jarrell. Edited and with an introduction by Brad Leithauser. New York: HarperCollins, 1995.

McCarthy, Mary. Intellectual Memoirs. New York: Harcourt Brace Jovanovich, 1992.

Shapiro, Karl. "What Is Not Poetry?" In Defense of Ignorance. New York: Random House, 1960.

Shelley, Percy Bysshe. "Julian and Maddalo: A Conversation." The New Shelley: Later Twentieth-Century Views. Edited by G. Kim Blank. New York: St. Martin's Press, 1991.

Yeats, W. B. Essays and Introductions. New York: Macmillan, 1961.

I WAS A TEENAGE BEATNIK

Beckett, Samuel. Krapp's Last Tape. (Sound recording) Spoken Arts 788, 1961. Also, (videocassette) directed by Alan Schneider, produced by H.B. Lutz and Mark Wright. New York: Pennebaker Associates, 1988.

Céline, Louis-Ferdinand. Journey to the End of the Night. New York: New Directions, 1983.

Cervantes, Miguel de. Don Quixote: A New Translation. Edith Grossman. Introduction by Harold Bloom. New York: Ecco, 2003. First published by Francisco de Robles, 1605.

Ferlinghetti, Lawrence. A Coney Island of the Mind. New York: New

Directions, 1968.

Hall, Radclyffe. *The Well of Loneliness*. Garden City, NY: Sundial Press, 1928.

Johnson, Joyce. *Minor Characters*. Boston: Houghton Mifflin, 1983.

Joyce, James. *Ulysses*. New York: Random House, 1946.

Kerouac, Jack. *The Dharma Bums*. New York: Viking Press, 1958.

Patchen, Kenneth. *The Journal of Albion Moonlight*. New York: The United Book Guild, 1944.

Toomer, Jean. *Cane*. Foreword by Waldo Frank. New York: Boni and Liveright, 1923.

THE MEANING OF GUILT

Tyler, Anne. *Saint Maybe*. New York: Knopf, 1991.

SELF AND STRANGENESS

Beauvoir, Simone de. *The Second Sex*. Edited and translated by H.M. Parshley. New York: Knopf, 1971, c1952.

Cherry, Kelly. *Augusta Played*. Boston: Houghton Mifflin, 1979; Baton Rouge: Louisiana State University Press, 1998.

Eugenides, Jeffrey. *Middlesex*. New York: Farrar, Straus and Giroux, 2002.

Keats, John. Letter to George and Thomas Keats dated Sunday, 22 December 1817. *The Letters of John Keats, 1814-1821*. Edited by Hyder Edward Rollins. Cambridge: Harvard University Press, 1999, 1958.

Russ, Joanna. "What Can a Heroine Do? Or Why Women Can't Write." *To Write Like a Woman: Essays in Feminism and Science Fiction*. Bloomington: Indiana University Press, 1995.

FICTIONS BY FOUR CONTEMPORARY AFRICAN AMERICAN AUTHORS

Dove, Rita. *Through the Ivory Gate*. New York: Pantheon Books, 1992.

Jones, Gayl. *Corregidora*. New York: Random House, 1975; Boston: Beacon Press, 1986.

McElroy, Colleen J. *Jesus and Fat Tuesday and Other Short Stories*. Berkeley: Creative Arts Book Co., 1987.

Shange, Ntozake. *Liliane: Resurrection of the Daughter*. New York: St. Martin's Press, 1994.

_____. *For Colored Girls Who Have Considered Suicide When the Rainbow is Enuf*. DVD. West Long Branch, NJ: Kultur, 2002.

_____. *Sassafras, Cypress & Indigo*. New York: St. Martin's Press, 1982.

ART WE CANNOT LIVE WITHOUT

Brown, Mary Ward. *It Wasn't All Dancing*. Tuscaloosa: University of Alabama Press, 2002.

_____. *Tongues of Flame*. New York: E. P. Dutton, 1986; University of Alabama Press, 2001.

Chekhov, Anton. "The Kiss." *The Stories of Anton Tchekov*. Edited, with an introduction, by Robert N. Linscott. New York: The Modern Library, 1932; Whitefish, MT: Kessinger Publishing, 2005.

SELF AND SENSIBILITY: ELIZABETH HARDWICK

Adler, Renata. *Speedboat*. New York: Random House, 1976.

Donoghue, Denis. "Big Effects and Hard-Worked Perceptions." Review of *Bartleby in Manhattan by Elizabeth Hardwick*. *The New York Times*, 12 June 1983.

Dreiser, Theodore. *An American Tragedy*. New York: Library of America: Distributed to the trade in the U.S. by Penguin Putnam, 2003.

Hardwick, Elizabeth. "The Apotheosis of Martin Luther King," "The Oswald Family," and "The Sense of the Presence." *Bartleby in Manhattan and Other Essays*. New York: Random House, 1983.

_____. *Best American Essays 1986*. Introduction. Boston: Houghton Mifflin, 1987.

_____. *The Ghostly Lover*. Afterword. New York: Harcourt, Brace and Co., 1945; Ecco Press, 1982, 1989.

_____. "Bloomsbury and Virginia Woolf," "Seduction and Betrayal," and "Sylvia Plath." *Seduction and Betrayal: Women and Literature*. New York, Random House 1974.

_____. *Sight-readings: American Fictions*. New York: Random House, 1998.

_____. *The Simple Truth*. New York: Harcourt, Brace, 1955.

_____. *Sleepless Nights*. New York: Random House, 1979.

_____. "Anderson, Millay and Crane in Their Letters." *A View of My Own: Essays in Literature and Society*. New York: Noonday Press, 1963.

Hughes, Ted. *The Birthday Letters*. New York: Farrar, Straus, and Giroux, 1998.

Lowell, Robert. "Man and Wife." *Life Studies*. New York: Farrar, Straus, and Cudahy, 1959.

LITERARY THEORY AND THE ACTUAL WRITER
Bloom, Harold. *The Anxiety of Influence: A Theory of Poetry*. New
York: Oxford University Press, 1997.

THE DARESOMENESS OF A SOUTHERN WOMAN
Mason, Bobbie Ann. *Clear Springs: A Memoir*. New York: Random
House, 1999.

A GIRL IN A LIBRARY
Brooks, James L. 1987. *Broadcast News*, 35 mm, 133 min. Twentieth
Century Fox Film Corporation. Videocassette.
Chappell, Fred. "Ideally Grasping the Actual Flower" and "Proposition
IVa." *First and Last Words: Poems*. Baton Rouge: Louisiana State
University Press, 1989.
Humes, Harry. *Winter Weeds: Poems*. Columbia: University of
Missouri, 1983.
Jarrell, Randall. "A Girl in a Library." *Selected Poems*. New York: Knopf,
1955.
Root, William Pitt. "Holocaust." *The Greensboro Review* 1.1 (1966).
Also, *The Beloit Poetry Journal* 16.1 (1965).
Watson, Robert. *A Paper Horse: Poems*. New York: Atheneum, 1962.

TWO FEUILLETONS
Kizer, Carolyn. *One Hundred Great Poems by Women*. Hopewell, N.J.:
Ecco Press, 1995.

THE GLOBE AND THE BRAIN
Hemingway, Ernest. "Hills like White Elephants." *Men Without
Women*. New York: C. Scribner's Sons, 1927.
Rubin, Jr., Louis D. *Where the Southern Cross the Yellow Dog*.
Columbia: University of Missouri Press, 2005.
Stegner, Wallace. "Sense of Place." *Where the Bluebird Sings to the
Lemonade Springs: Living and Writing in the West*. New York:
Random House, 1992.
Welty, Eudora. *Place in Fiction*. New York: House of Books, 1957. Also,
The Eye of the Story: Selected Essays and Reviews. Eudora Welty.
New York: Vintage Books, 1979, c1978.
_____. "Powerhouse." *A Curtain of Green*. New York: Harcourt,

Brace, & World, Inc., 1936.

_____. "A Still Moment." *The Wide Net and Other Stories.*
New York: Harcourt, Brace and Company, 1943.

WHAT COMES NEXT

Cisneros, Sandra. "Hairs." *The House on Mango Street.* Houston, TX:
Arte Público Press, 1984; New York: Vintage Books, 1991; New
York: Knopf, 1994.

Eliot, T. S. *The Sacred Wood: Essays on Poetry and Criticism.* London:
Methuen, 1920; New York: Knopf, 1930.

Gordon, Mary. "The Parable of the Cave or: In Praise of Watercolors."
The Writer on Her Work. Edited by Janet Sternburg. New York: W.
W. Norton, 1980.

Gowdy, Barbara. *We So Seldom Look on Love.* Toronto: Somerville
House, 1992; South Royalton, VT: Steerforth Press, 1997.

Hempel, Amy. "In the Cemetery Where Al Jolson Is Buried." *Reasons to
Live: Stories.* New York: Knopf, 1985; HarperPerennial, 1995.

Houston, Pam. *Cowboys Are My Weakness.* New York: W.W. Norton,
1992; New York: Washington Square Press, 1992.

McElroy, Colleen J. *Jesus and Fat Tuesday and Other Short Stories.*
Berkeley: Creative Arts Book Co., 1987.

Minot, Susan. "Last." *Lust and Other Stories.* Boston: Houghton
Mifflin/S. Lawrence, 1989.

Oates, Joyce Carol. "Where Are You Going, Where Have You Been?"
*Where Are You Going, Where Have You been? Stories of Young
America.* Greenwich, Connecticut: Fawcett Publications, 1974.

Ozick, Cynthia. *The Shawl.* New York: Knopf, 1989.

Paley, Grace. "The Long-Distance Runner." *Enormous Changes at the
Last Minute.* New York: Farrar, Straus, Giroux, 1974.

_____. "Mother." *Later the Same Day.* New York: Farrar,
Straus, Giroux, 1985.

Phillips, Jayne Anne. "Souvenir." *Black Tickets.* New York: Delacorte
Press/S. Lawrence, 1979.

Schulman, Helen. "Pushing the Point." *Not a Free Show: Stories.* New
York: Knopf, 1988.

Welty, Eudora. "Why I live at the P.O." *A Curtain of Green.* New York:
Harcourt, Brace, & World, Inc., 1936.

WHY I WRITE NOW

Faulkner, William. Nobel Speech delivered on December 10, 1950 in

Stockholm, Sweden. Print: Rochester, N.Y.: Press of the Good Mountain, 1951.

CALLED TO IT

Cherry, Kelly. *Augusta Played.* Boston: Houghton Mifflin, 1979; Baton Rouge: Louisiana State University Press, 1998.

_____. *Death and Transfiguration.* Baton Rouge: Louisiana State University Press, 1997.

_____. *The Exiled Heart: A Meditative Autobiography.* Baton Rouge: Louisiana State University Press, 1991.

_____. *God's Loud Hand: Poems.* Baton Rouge: Louisiana State University Press, 1993.

_____. "What Is Poetry? What Is Music?" *History, Passion, Freedom, Death, and Hope: Prose about Poetry.* Florida: University of Tampa Press, 2006.

_____. *In the Wink of an Eye.* San Diego: Harcourt Brace Jovanovich, 1983.

_____. *My Life and Dr. Joyce Brothers: A Novel in Stories.* Chapel Hill, NC: Algonquin Books of Chapel Hill, 1990; Tuscaloosa: University of Alabama Press, 2004.

_____. *Natural Theology: Poems.* Baton Rouge: Louisiana State University Press, 1988.

_____. *Rising Venus: Poems.* Baton Rouge: Louisiana State University Press, 2002.

_____. *Writing the World.* Columbia: University of Missouri Press, 1995.

Dove, Rita. "Rita Dove." *Contemporary Authors Autobiography Series.*

Garrett, George, ed. *The Girl in the Black Raincoat.* New York: Duell, Sloan & Pearce, 1966.

INDEX

Kelly Cherry is the author of nineteen books of poetry, novels, short stories, criticism, and memoir—including this year's *Girl in a Library: On Women Writers and the Writing Life* and *The Retreats of Thought: Poems*—eight chapbooks, and two translations of classical plays. Her short fiction has appeared in *Best American Short Stories, Prize Stories: The O. Henry Awards, The Pushcart Prize,* and *New Stories from the South,* and her collection *The Society of Friends: Stories* received the Dictionary of Literary Biography Award in 2000 for the best short story collection of 1999. For her body of work in poetry she has received the Hanes Prize from the Fellowship of Southern Writers. She is Eudora Welty Professor Emerita of English and Evjue-Bascom Professor Emerita in the Humanities at the University of Wisconsin, Madison, and has held named chairs and distinguished visiting writer positions at a number of universities. She and her husband, Burke Davis III, live on a small farm in Virginia with their two dogs.